"Karen Sebastian grants permission to experience mourning. Her personal stories make no judgement calls on another person's grief. And the Hope Tools are practical and gentle on the soul. I am deeply touched by her metaphor of riding the waves of grief."

~ Rev. Cassie Wade
United Methodist Pastor

"Author and speaker Karen Sebastian taps the depths of her heart and soul to draw out jewels of wisdom from her own experiences during and after the death of her dear husband and lifelong partner, Bill. Her personal journey offers hope and inspiration for those of us who have suffered the absence of loved ones in our lives and wrestle with our own painful questions."

~ Rev. Dennison Strong
Missionary-Evangelist

"In this book, Karen reminds us of how important it is to increase hope so that we have strength, joy, direction, and balance throughout our amazing journey as we navigate through the many storms of life. Even in the darkest nights of grief, hope is there to remind us of and guide us into the arms of the One who knows our end from the beginning."

~ Lynn Wilford Scarborough
Author of *Talk Like Jesus*

THE POWER OF

# HOPE

IN MOURNING

*RIDE THE WAVES TO COMFORT*

## KAREN SEBASTIAN

harrishousepublishing.com

THE POWER OF HOPE IN MOURNING: RIDE THE WAVES TO COMFORT
Copyright © 2015 by Karen Sebastian
Published by Harris House Publishing
www.harrishousepublishing.com
Colleyville, Texas
USA

*Cover by Christopher Flynn*
*Cover photo © Ahmed Mahin Fayaz*
*Author's photo by Lynn Scarborough*

**Library of Congress Cataloging-in-Publication Data**
Sebastian, Karen.
        The power of hope in mourning : ride the waves to comfort /
        Karen Sebastian.
               pages cm
        ISBN 978-0-9862831-2-3 (pbk.)
        1. Grief— Religious aspects.  2. Bereavement—Psychological aspects.
        3. Loss (Psychology)  4. Hope— Religious aspects.  I. Title
BF575.G7 S43     2015
155.9`37—dc23

                          2015946656

# Dedication

To my dad, Bill Pritchett. You taught me through example how to trust God in so many ways as I was growing up. Then when Mom died a few years ago, I learned even more as you mourned the death of your life partner who had been by your side for over three quarters of a century. Your hope in the Lord is my steady inspiration to keep moving forward to embrace all aspects of mourning with the confidence that joy does come in the morning.

# Acknowledgements

**To my husband, Bill:** Despite his own physical struggles, he was my constant cheerleader and spoke often of the awesome plan God had for our lives. I'm eternally grateful I was able to share ups and downs, tears and laughter, challenges and breakthroughs, healthy times and the grace he showed even with serious health issues. Bill embodied hope through steadfastness in the midst of his suffering and never wavered in his steady encouragement for me to continue believing in big dreams.

**To my children, Elizabeth, Eliberto, Megan, Jacob, Sean, and Sarah:** Thank you for your support as I wrote this book. You have taught me more than you will ever imagine about how we all mourn in our own way and at our own pace. Thank you for mingling your tears with mine as we celebrate the legacy of your dad—a truly great man.

**To my grandsons, Donovan, Devin, Davon, Dominic, and Levi:** What joy you brought to your Papa Bill's heart! I am so grateful your early years have memories of his wise words and love. He would be proud of the amazing men you are becoming.

**To my granddaughters, Viola and Ellie:** I am sad to know that you will not ever get to experience a Papa Bill hug, yet I know that the same generational blessings rest on you. You light up my life and give me hope for the future.

**To my sister, Linda Richey:** Thank you for your support and spiritual insights. Having you as a sister makes me feel rich.

**To Refuge, my church family:** Thank you for walking beside me during this difficult season. Your prayer support and prophetic insight have been hope rays just when I most needed them.

**To all my precious friends who have prayed and encouraged me since Bill's death:** There is not enough room to list each of you. You have enriched my life and I treasure your friendship.

**To Terry Harris and Harris House Publishing:** Thank you for believing in this message of hope. I appreciate your expertise and most of all your heart.

# Contents

# Foreword

*By Rev. G. Marie Brown,*
*Relational Care Pastor, Gateway Church*

From the time I was very young, I remember seeing families, including my own extended family members, walk through very difficult times of grief when a loved one died. My grandfather and father were both pastors, and helping people during times of loss was just part of our life in the parsonage. I never learned to fear death in those experiences, but I did learn just how shocking and devastating loss could be, especially in the weeks and months following the death. Even as a child, when I saw the pain people experienced, I wanted to help them find comfort, but I felt helpless to do anything beyond offering a kind word or expression of love.

During these last eight years at Gateway Church (Southlake, Texas), where my role has been in the area of pastoral care ministry, I have walked with grieving families continually. Our average weekly attendance is around 30,000, so helping families navigate death, funerals, and their ongoing grief journey is a part of my daily assignment. I love what I do because it allows me to minister the compassion, love, comfort, and peace of our Lord! But walking with people through very difficult and dark days can be a daunting endeavor still. Even when the death is not sudden or traumatic, people often cannot find their way to a healthy grieving journey.

I am always so grateful when I find an excellent tool that can help the grieving heart find that path to productive mourning. We know God freely gives His comfort, peace, and newfound joy, but how can we help people connect to this provision? When their hearts are broken and torn between realizing they must move forward, but not having the courage to take those first steps, people need a bridge. A bridge that helps them walk over to a new understanding and awareness of God's grace, which is always given during the season of mourning.

*The Power of Hope in Mourning* is such a bridge which will minister to broken hearts. In her book, Karen captures the dilemma all of us face as we contemplate how to handle grief. None of us readily accept this unwanted path, and yet experience tells us death is as much a part of life as breathing. So how can we move forward? How can we move beyond the paralyzing reality that our life will never be the same because that one we loved so much is no longer there with us?

What I love about *The Power of Hope in Mourning* is the practical approach Karen uses. It applies and relates so well to our day-to-day—and even sometimes our moment-to-moment—grief journey that we must embrace, no matter how resistant our hearts are to our new reality. We must move toward our future, but everything in our hearts is pulling us back to the past where our loved one still exists in our memories. This is the reluctant journey Karen so aptly helps us navigate. Like an experienced instructor in any given art, because Karen draws from her own grief journey, her ability to help others navigate is masterful.

"Riding the waves" alongside her careful, thoughtful, and loving guidance does allow us to relax, knowing God is right there with us. Instead of being knocked down by those waves of grief, we can lay back and relax in His arms, knowing He will never allow us to sink. She teaches us to embrace the ride, not resist it. In doing so, she gives us permission to let our grief flow out freely. We learn to trust God, because each time we pour our hearts out to Him, He is right there—helping us ride the waves and always answering us, even in our most painful life experiences.

Her guidance, supported by the examples from her own journey, is the ideal blend of practical advice and deep spiritual wisdom all wrapped up in the perfect package for those who mourn. That package is HOPE! It should be easy to find, and yet it so often eludes those who are mourning. Karen's masterful guideposts help us move toward the power of hope by helping us realize it is the answer to our deepest fears, our long-held regrets, our inconsolable sorrow, and our overwhelming sense of loss. Hope is the path which allows us to be released and find the future God has for each of us.

# Introduction

*Blessed are those who mourn for they will be comforted.*
*Matthew 5:4*

This is a great promise for those who feel like they are drowning in a sea of sorrow after the death of a loved one. I know what it is to mourn. I experienced it when my mother died and then two years later when my husband died in his sleep. In the Sermon on the Mount, Jesus said, "Blessed (happy, fortunate, to be envied) are those who mourn for they shall be comforted." I don't know about you, but I don't envy those who have a reason to mourn. The blessing doesn't come in the reason to mourn, but in the level of comfort we receive when we allow ourselves to embrace our grief.

One of the reasons that we struggle with connecting blessing and grieving is that we lose hope in the face of death. Most people are, at best, uncomfortable with the concept of death. We know it's an inevitable part of life as it says in Ecclesiastes 3:1-2, "There is a time for everything, and a season for every activity under the heavens: a time to be born and a time to die."

Most of us don't want to think about death and how it could affect us and our families. When someone faces the death of someone they love, we don't know what to say, so we avoid the person or, worse yet, say something that adds to their pain. As Christians, we are particularly impatient with those who seem to linger in the dark valley of despair. We quote scriptures and offer platitudes that fall flat to the one who feels like their world has just collapsed.

This book is about finding hope in the midst of an ocean of deep pain and sorrow. Hope reassures us that, when someone we love dies, the Lord sustains us and comforts us even when we feel like we may never recover. Some stay on the beach and never venture out to the depth of their feelings. They numb the pain and push it down. The danger with that approach is that the waves build up and then hit all at once with the devastating force of a tsunami. Others swim out to deep waters where they feel like they are going under and are exhausted from treading water. Feeling alone and desperate, they want to give up.

You will receive comfort as you choose to mourn completely and fully rather than rushing the process. First of all, there is no cookie cutter method of mourning. Every individual has a unique approach, and each relationship is different. Secondly, grieving properly takes work and an intentional purpose to keep walking through the darkness without wavering because we know that we do not have to fear—for God is with us, His rod and His staff comfort us (Psalm 23:4). Finally, there is always hope, even when you feel like the water is too deep and you are sinking. In Deuteronomy 33:27, we read, "The eternal God is your refuge, and underneath are the everlasting arms." Because of that truth, when the waves come, you can learn the art of riding them all the way to shore where you will find His comfort.

Hope allows you to dream of a future filled with precious memories of the past, happiness in the present, and great days ahead. Right now, it may be hard to believe that you will ever feel that again because your heart is broken. Cling to the hope and the stories of others who have continued to move forward even as the shadows loom in the valley of the shadow of death.

This book is designed in such a way that you can read the entire book from start to finish or you can pick a chapter that appeals to you at this moment. After a short personal anecdote or Bible story, you will find practical suggestions called Hope Tools which will help you in your grief journey. These were gleaned from my experiences while grieving the deaths of my mother and my husband. Following these suggestions are scripture-based prayers that will build your faith and increase your hope. Choose and practice using the tools that appeal to you. Please share with others who are embarking on their own grief journey and add your personal story, as it will be a great encouragement to them.

# Riding the Waves

I was in the fifth grade when my parents became missionaries in the small Central American country of Costa Rica. One of my fondest memories as a child was spending time at the beach. We would drive down the winding road from the capital city of San Jose to Puntarenas, a small port town on the Pacific coast. At that time, it was filled with fishermen and their families. Most tourists had not yet discovered this tropical paradise with its warm, gentle waves and swaying palm trees.

"Would you like to go to Puntarenas with me?" my dad asked. "I have to check on the church down there."

My ears perked up. I loved going to the beach.

"I would love to go with you, Daddy," I replied excitedly. "Will we have time to go the beach?"

"After I finish talking with some of the pastors, we can go down to the beach and get in the water," he said.

As promised, when he had finished his meetings, we walked down to the beach. Daddy loved to body surf. Usually my brother Darrell joined him in the water while I was content at the water's edge, building castles with the wet sand. But Darrell had not come on this trip.

Daddy strolled out into the waist deep water. "Why don't you come on out in the water with me?" he yelled over the surf. "Did I ever teach you how to float?" he asked.

"I tried one time in the pool. I did pretty good until Darrell pulled me under the water," I said timidly.

He rode a wave over to me and finally coaxed me out into the water.

"Just relax and trust that the water will hold you. See, like this." With those words of advice, he lay back in the water. I stood in the waist high waves, wishing I could relax.

"I'm scared, Daddy!" I cried.

"Here, let me show you how," he replied. He came over to me and gently said, "Here you go. Just lie back on the water. You can do this."

He then placed his strong hand in the hollow of my back. With that reassuring touch, I leaned back.

"Now relax," he said. "I've got you. I won't let you go under."

I leaned back and tried to relax. I had done this recently in a swimming pool with a certain amount of success. The ocean was different, though, because it was in perpetual motion. I would start to sink when I tensed up. I began to relax when I could feel my dad's strong hand supporting me. Just then, a wave came and separated me from that supporting hand. A feeling of panic gripped my heart when I realized that, at the peak of the wave, my feet could not touch the ocean floor. I was in over my head, yet could hear my dad's reassuring voice.

"Keep relaxing, pumpkin," he said. "You're doing great."

It took everything in me to make myself relax. I splashed a little as I reclined and leaned into the water. For one second, my head went under water and then bobbed back up. I was floating on my own. I had conquered my fear.

## Taking On the Next Stage

Little did I know the plans Dad had for me. I thought that learning to float was surely enough for one visit to the beach. The next afternoon when we went back to the beach, Dad was determined to have a partner with whom he could body surf. With the confidence of a competent 'floater,' I showed off being able to lay back and pretend the ocean was a soft mattress. I moved into the next phase of my instruction, which was to learn how to tread water. This one wasn't so simple, because it involved timing and many variables. When treading water, you move your feet like you're riding a bike. This was important as I learned to wait for the perfect wave. You turned to your side and looked back at the waves that were coming. The key factor was to learn to identify a great wave. The beauty of Puntarenas was that the waves were small and the water was warm.

You could do one of three things when a wave was coming: (1) keep treading water and wait for the next one; (2) relax and go under the water; or (3) swim like crazy in order to 'catch the wave' and then ride it to the shore.

So began my efforts to improve my timing and gain body surfing skills. It was a quest to catch the wave just right and make it all the way to the shore. One time when I made it in just fine, I was caught in a cross-current which pounded my head into the sand with each wave. It was scary yet exhilarating.

## RIDE THE WAVES OF GRIEF

I didn't realize how vital Dad's lessons would be to me . . . until my Heavenly Father taught me how to apply them to a grieving heart. My mother died in her sleep early one Monday morning after a short time in hospice. It was the week before her 91st birthday, and I was planning to visit her when I finished conducting some training seminars in Kansas. As my flight landed at the Denver airport, I glanced at my phone and saw a missed call from my husband. I decided to wait to call him back until I reached the gate for my next flight, but our son Sean called me as I walked through the terminal.

"Mom, I have bad news. You might want to sit down for this," he admonished kindly.

Fear gripped the pit of my stomach as I reached for the nearest seat I could find. "Is everyone okay?" I asked.

"Mom, Grams died last night. She just didn't wake up," he said sadly. "I'm so sorry to have to give you this bad news over the phone."

Feeling like a wave of cold water hit me in the face, I sobbed quietly for a few minutes before I managed to compose myself. When I could talk again, I called my husband and my supervisor to let them know that I was going to just go ahead and travel to California to support Dad instead of going to the training. It was a huge relief to have made this quick decision and to feel full support from my supervisor.

After rebooking my ticket, I sank into an empty seat at the gate for my upcoming flight. A wave of grief washed over me, and as I relaxed, my tears started to flow. I didn't try to hold them back. Instead, I let myself feel the deep sadness that on this earth I would never again feel Mom's hug or hear her sweet voice.

## All Is Well

At Mom's funeral service, we sang one of her favorite hymns, "It Is Well with My Soul." Here are the words (along with my personal interpretation in parentheses):

*When peace, like a river, attendeth my way*
*(When my life is peaceful and everything is going my way),*
*When sorrows like sea billows roll*
*(When sadness comes at me like the surge of huge waves),*
*Whatever my lot, Thou has taught me to say*
*(No matter what circumstances I face, You have taught me to say),*
*It is well with my soul.*

This song kept playing repeatedly in my head, and so I researched the story behind these powerful words written by Horatio Spafford. He was a wealthy attorney who, much like a modern-day Job, had everything going well in the beginning of his life. Then, he and his family suffered one tragedy after another. His son died of scarlet fever. He lost a fortune in real estate in the Chicago fire. He sent his wife and four daughters on holiday to Europe while he stayed behind to take care of some last minute business. Their ship sank and all of his daughters were lost at sea. As he traveled to bring his wife home, he wrote these powerful words. It is told that the captain of his ship was able to pinpoint the spot where their ship sank. It was an area where the ocean is three miles deep. No wonder he described his overwhelming grief as a surging wave.

I spent a week with my dad after Mom's service. I don't even remember exactly how we started 'riding the waves.' By the end of that week, though, we had perfected a wonderful grieving technique that brought us to comfort when a wave of sorrow would randomly hit. The one who was feeling the impact of the wave of sorrow would go get the other one by the hand. We would then sit in the matching recliners in their small living room and pray together as the one feeling the sadness would feel the surge of emotion and then watch it subside, much like the motion of a wave as it moves toward the shore. We would then share a favorite saying, comment, or anecdote. Usually we ended up laughing. Just like when we went body surfing all those years ago, it was much more fun to have a buddy.

# *Hope Tools*

## FOCUS ON MOURNING

The many details to take care of and emotions to process when a loved one dies can seem overwhelming. Much like being stuck in an ocean, another wave begins to surge just as you adjust to the one that hit you. Grieving is hard work and requires a commitment to honestly express what you feel. Make a commitment to see the process all the way through. This can be hard because, in the beginning of the grieving process, the pain may feel too great to bear. As darkness surrounds us, it is easy to panic and want to run from it all. Hope becomes the light that guides us through this dark storm. There is an end in sight even though it may not feel like it right now.

When I was a child, we had competitions to see who could say the most Bible verses. Everyone wanted to be the one who quoted the shortest verse in the Bible, found in John 11:35, "Jesus wept." This verse may be short, but it is also profound. Our Lord allowed Himself to feel the sorrow of the death of His friend Lazarus. He modeled transparency by fully embracing what He was feeling.

Give yourself permission to do the same. Grieving has a purpose and a place. Sadness is an honest emotion, and tears can be cleansing.

## MANAGE WAVE SURGES

Grieving can be unpredictable. It's best to handle each wave as it comes. These waves may come unexpectedly and at inconvenient times. Take a few minutes to process when a wave of grief hits you. Give yourself permission to cry. Relax even as you feel a momentary loss of control. It usually passes quickly as you let it wash over you. You have God's promises that He is always with you and will not let you go under. When you are feeling overwhelmed, remember God's promise in Isaiah 43:2, "When you pass through the waters, I will be with you; and when you pass through the rivers, they will not sweep over you."

Other times you can ride the wave all the way to the shore. After my husband died, waves of grief hit me unexpectedly, but as I allowed myself to feel the sorrow and took the time to process the reason that I missed him, a warm memory would surface that left me smiling. I felt great comfort as I enjoyed the richness of sweet memories.

## Let Others Know What to Expect

Many who are grieving apologize for their tears because they fear that they are making others feel uncomfortable. Others may ask why you are still crying and want to distract you from the process. One of the best things for me was to explain that I was not ever certain when a wave of grief would come over me. I used the phrase "I'm feeling a wave." My eyes would usually fill with tears, and I would take a minute to process what I was feeling. In this simple way, I was giving myself permission to grieve and releasing others to do the same.

Write out your script so you know the main points you need to make in order to express your coping process to others. Personalize it and let those you love the most know how they can support you during this time. By doing this, you set those around you free from the awkward feeling they might experience when wondering what to do with your display of emotions. I learned to relax and stop apologizing for the tears. Here's a sample of the script:

"Since your Dad died, I have been on a very different grief journey. My emotions are completely unpredictable. The tears come when I least expect them. (Give an example, such as, 'The other day I was crying in the pickle aisle of the grocery store.') I promise to let you know when this is happening by using the term 'I'm getting hit by a wave.' At that point, all you need to do is to give me a moment to feel the emotions, cry a few tears, and get right back on track. I find that when I relax, I can 'ride the wave' and often relive a wonderful memory with Dad. Please let me know if you need the same space to mourn."

It is a comfort to know that others have walked this path before me and have been able to come out on the other end stronger. When we share our hurt with someone else, it doesn't feel as heavy. In this process of explaining your approach to mourning, avoid common words used for waves of grief such as ambushed, bushwhacked, overcome, etc. Instead, let others know that you are embracing this grieving process and leaning into the Lord as you feel the pain. If they are willing to do so, teach those close to you how to ride the waves to comfort. Your example of embracing what you're feeling and processing your sorrow can become a powerful example they can follow.

## TREAD WATER

Early mornings were hard for me in the weeks immediately following my husband's death. I kept busy during the day and was usually surrounded by people. However, in the dim hours before dawn as I was waking, my feelings seemed most vulnerable. Some mornings I woke up sobbing. After having a good cry, I would gather all the sadness and offer it up to the Lord. Other days, I would feel deep sadness and despair, yet seemed to have no tears. I would pull out the sympathy cards that I had received and read them slowly. The temporary paralysis would lift, and I felt able to face my day.

As much as you want life to stop after your loved one dies, it does not. Sometimes you can hardly even catch your breath because there is so much to do. And so you just keep moving while making funeral arrangements, writing the obituary, etc. It can seem like you are stuck in one spot and barely able to keep your head above water. All the activities tend to keep you distracted and then there is a huge letdown once everyone else returns to their normal routine and lives.

During this process of mourning, you may feel exhausted for no apparent reason. Grieving requires a great deal of emotional energy, so give yourself extra space to rest and process what you're feeling. At the same time, avoid complete isolation. Returning to a regular schedule can be hard at first, but can also help to re-establish a sense of order. As you return to regular life, keep in mind that the condition of your heart is the key to keeping your head above water. When you feel angry, be sure to find ways to express it openly in a healthy way and to resolve it. Let the tears flow freely as you ride each wave. Once the wave reaches the shore, you may even enjoy a few chuckles as you relish the good memories.

## PRAYER

Lord, give me the grace to embrace the pain that I am feeling right now instead of numbing out. Grant me hope to know that these waves of grief will not last forever as I pray and get Your perspective (Colossians 3:2 MSG). I am grateful that You hear my groaning and rise up to throw me a lifeline so You can pull me to a safe place. This is what I long for and I know You will not disappoint me (Psalms 12:5 NASB).

Teach me what Your comfort looks like so I can find the blessings hidden there. You say that You are very close to the brokenhearted, yet I can't always feel Your presence (Psalm 34:18). That's when I trust that no matter where I go, You are there with me, leading me (Psalm 139:10).

I choose to put my hope in You when a wave of grief washes over me. I will hold my breath with full confidence that I will come up for air and even learn to ride the waves to comfort. Thank You for Your promises to comfort me as I choose to mourn completely and fully. I swim out to the deep end of the waters, knowing that You will sustain me and support me (Colossians 3:2). I can always depend on Your faithfulness to uphold me with Your right hand (Isaiah 41:10).

In Jesus' name. Amen.

## Hope Expressions

*Don't be afraid, I've redeemed you. I've called your name. You're mine. When you're in over your head, I'll be there with you. When you're in rough waters, you will not go down. When you're between a rock and a hard place, it won't be a dead end.*
*Isaiah 43:2-4 MSG*

# Getting 'The Call'

Miracles happen every day; we just don't see them. When you get the 'call' that changes your life forever, time seems to stop, and you slow down enough to appreciate the events that make that day memorable and miraculous.

The journey that brought me to this day had been a long one. Bill, my husband, grew up knowing that he was different physically than the other kids, but was not quite sure how. He only knew he had to work harder than anyone else to make it through the day. When he was a teenager, the other kids and even his P.E. coach made fun of his 'wings' as he did his push-ups and attempted to climb the rope in gym class. He took it all in stride and found workarounds. Determined to build up his muscles, he lifted weights regularly.

After we married, I noticed that no matter how hard he exercised, each workout was like his first. In spite of that, he continued to exercise diligently. He never complained about this because it was all he had ever known. He found alternatives and didn't let anything stop him. This persistent approach to hurdles served him well his entire life. When we moved to Texas, however, the summer heat further wiped him out. We thought it was because he had suffered a heat stroke a few years earlier. I took a full-time job to provide health insurance while Bill devoted his energy to being the pastor of a small church. I was increasingly angry about how he did less and less to help around the house and especially with the yard work. I thought he was just discouraged and needed to try harder.

## A Difficult Path

A visit to the emergency room with chest pains and a week in the hospital showed that, while he had not had a heart attack, there was something going on with his muscles. A lady in our church worked for a neurologist, and she encouraged us to set up an appointment. They did a muscle biopsy that gave us a devastating diagnosis—Muscular Dystrophy. Based on that information, we set up an appointment at the MDA clinic at UT Southwestern Medical Center. We had been to many doctors who weren't able to give Bill a definitive diagnosis. At least now we knew what we were facing.

Dr. Nations entered the room and smiled at us. "Mr. Sebastian, please take off your shoes and shirt. Then, please walk across the floor on your heels," she said kindly.

He tried to do it several times but could not keep his balance. I watched in horror as I saw the degree of his limitations. I lived with the man, and yet was unaware of how hard he had to work to make it through a normal day.

"You have Facio Scapulo Humeral Dystrophy (FSHD). We will do further tests to confirm this diagnosis," she stated. "The heat will particularly deplete your energy."

She turned toward me and said, "Just to give you some perspective, Mrs. Sebastian, if he does yard work in this Texas summer heat, he feels the same as you would if you ran a marathon without advance training and preparation."

My eyes filled with tears as the full impact of what she was saying hit me. I realized for the first time how hard Bill had to work in order to do things that most of us took for granted. He never complained, so I had no idea how difficult getting through an average day was for him, particularly in the heat. He would say in the years after that appointment that he felt like a big weight lifted off of his back that day. He got me off his back.

Over the next eleven years, Bill's strength continued to decline gradually. Like the growth of your children, you don't notice changes until you look at old pictures or put a new mark on the doorpost. One weakness we could not ignore was when Bill stopped swallowing. A swallowing test showed that the epiglottis was not doing its job of closing when he swallowed. This lack of coordination made it hard for him to even swallow his own saliva. He also had more and more trouble breathing.

Several weeks after the swallowing test, we were in the emergency room so Bill could get an IV to counteract severe dehydration. His condition was serious enough that his doctor admitted him into the hospital to put in a feeding tube. Unfortunately, they did not take his Muscular Dystrophy into account and tried to lay him flat on the operating table. This went on for several days as his condition deteriorated. Finally, he ended up in the ICU where they brought in the breathing specialists who were able to make the adjustments necessary to put in the feeding tube.

The ability to swallow never returned after his hospital stay. He would spend a major portion of his day suctioning his own saliva. Eventually, his diaphragm stopped working, so he depended on a ventilator to regulate his breathing. A pulmonary specialist encouraged him to get a tracheostomy because he was not getting enough oxygen through the facemask. My husband wrote "NO – thank you!" on his white board.

As we drove home from the doctor's office that day, I asked him why he wouldn't agree to get the trāch. Unable to speak because of the ventilator mask, he attempted to communicate through sign language. All I could get was, "I'm held." I finally gave up until we got home, and that's when he emphatically wrote in huge letters on his white board: "I'm HEALED." I would not realize the significance of that declaration until later.

I was in Mississippi conducting an early morning training class when my phone rang. It startled me because this entire trip my phone wouldn't hold a charge. I was communicating with Bill via Facebook and was planning to get a new phone when I got back home. In training seminars, I usually ask everyone to turn their cell phones to silent, but I didn't worry about mine because it had not been working. Imagine my surprise when it rang. Noticing that it was my daughter, I stepped outside the training room and took the call.

"Hi, sweetie, what's up?" I asked casually. "By some miracle my phone just decided to start working. I'm in the middle of teaching a class."

"Mom, Dad died last night!" she said abruptly and then started sobbing.

I felt like I had been punched in the stomach. I found a chair so I could sit down as I struggled to process what was happening.

I went back into my training class and told the participants that our class would be rescheduled because I just got the news that my husband had moved to Heaven during the night. They looked at me a little strangely until the reality of what I said sank in. Every single one of them hugged me on their way out of the classroom, and many told me they were praying for me. And here was yet another miracle.

## NEEDING A MIRACLE

I opened the car door and plopped down in the seat. Briefly, I put my head in my hands and prayed for guidance and strength.

"Lord, I need Your help to get to my kids," I whispered through tears. I was thankful for the first miracle that my phone rang and I was able to leave early, but I felt like I was a million miles away and needed a miracle to drive the three hours to the airport. Some participants in the training class had offered to drive me there, but I declined because I needed to be alone to begin processing what had happened.

It was now 9 a.m. I was three hours away from the nearest airport and needed to get there by 12 noon in order to catch the next flight home. I also had to fill the rental car with gas, return it, and get through security. Glancing at my cell phone, I saw that the battery was super low because it still was not holding a charge. I needed a miracle and wished for the ability to teleport myself.

I unfolded the printout of shorter directions that showed a faster way to get to the airport. I could have never imagined the day before when it was given to me how very important it would be. I was going to need all the help I could get to make the next plane back to Texas to be with my kids and grandkids.

Before I left, I said a quick prayer for protection as I sped to the airport. Reaching over to turn on the radio for the first time since I had rented this car, I found another miracle because it was set to K-LOVE, a Christian radio station. It started sprinkling as I pulled on to the main highway.

The very first song they played as I started my journey was "Blessed Be the Name of the Lord."

*Blessed be Your name*
*On the road marked with suffering,*
*Though there's pain in the offering,*
*Blessed be Your name.*
*Every blessing You pour out,*
*I'll turn back to praise.*
*When the darkness closes in, Lord,*
*Still I will say,*
*Blessed be the name of the Lord,*
*Blessed be Your name.*
*You give and take away,*
*My heart will choose to say,*
*Lord, blessed be Your name.*

This familiar song took on new meaning. It's easy to sing this song when all is well in your life and you're on the receiving end of blessings. Now I was on a new road marked with suffering and pain due to the death of my dear husband. He was the love of my life. He was the one who had learned, over our 39 years of marriage, to finish my sentences. He was my biggest cheerleader.

I've always spoken of the power of our will and the choices we make. This somehow seemed different. But it wasn't. Here I was, speeding down the road to get to my family. I had a choice to make during that trip—the same one I had faced over and over during the last decade as we dealt with my husband's illness. I could run from it. I could hide behind my anger and justify my resistance or I could choose to move through the pain of this dark time. It was still my choice. I could choose bitterness or I could give all I was feeling to the One who would give me just what I needed at this precise second.

"Lord, I'm not ready for this," I said between my tears. Even as those words escaped my mouth, I knew it was an excuse. The mercy and grace showered on me during the difficult times we'd faced recently had all been preparing me for the call this morning and the drive I was taking right now. As the chorus came around again, I started to sing with all my might, "You give and take away." I chose to bless the name of the Lord—even in this dark time. The painful knot in my chest dissolved as I sang.

At that precise second, I drove from the tree-lined highway into an open area where the sky seemed on fire with a beautiful heart-shaped cloud. A shaft of light was shining through a hole in the middle of it. It felt like I was driving right through it. I smiled as I remembered all the times that these brilliant rays of light (or 'hope rays' as I like to call them) had filled the sky just when I most needed to be reminded of God's care for me. I smiled and felt the close presence of the Lord.

"I will trust You, Lord, even now," I said softly. At that moment, I prayed a prayer of surrender and in response, I received just what I needed to keep going. Just when we think we can't keep going, we get exactly what we need in response to simple obedience. That's truly a miracle.

The next song that played on the radio was "I Can Only Imagine." This song is about how we cannot even imagine what those who go before us see when they get to Heaven. For the next hour and a half, it seemed like the entire playlist had been selected for me just for that trip.

I made it on time for my flight home. It was a small jet that had a row of single seats on one side. I was assigned to the one in the very back. I put on my sunglasses and quietly cried the entire way. Every time I closed my eyes, I saw the snapshot of the hope rays. This is a journey that I didn't think I was ready to start. There are many changes, and there is pain. Yet my heart will choose to say, "Blessed be the name of the Lord."

# Hope Tools

## POSTPONE MAJOR DECISIONS

Many go about grieving as a checklist or a set of stages. In that light, they want to quickly move on with their lives and get back to normal. While there is no going back to the way things were before your loved one(s) died, it is good to slow down the process and embrace what you are feeling. It can be a precious time of journaling the memories and processing the pain. Also, it's a wonderful time to re-evaluate the priorities of your life.

There are certain things you need to do immediately for legal reasons and others that you would do well to wait to do. For example, notifying the appropriate entities and planning the funeral or memorial cannot wait. Once things settle down, however, there are many more decisions to make. It is common for a widow or widower to feel overwhelmed when they feel like decisions are almost impossible to make without their spouse's input.

Make a list of all that needs to be done and ask for help. Don't be in a hurry to get rid of your loved one's belongings, sell your home, or move to another state, even if you have those around you who are pushing you to do so. Instead, if your finances permit, stay the course and wait until you are in a healthier state of mind before you move to a different place in your life.

I received great advice from a friend who became a widow several years ago. She suggested that I wait at least a year before making any big decisions such as selling the house. It's important to be able to sort through the emotions and have a clear mind to process the ramifications of your decisions.

Then, when the time is right, it is best to move forward with living your life. You have a life ahead of you. There are joys to experience, challenges to overcome, and love to enjoy. Find an accountability partner who can help you move forward in areas where you might get stuck. Ask for help when you need it.

## ANTICIPATE FIRSTS

The death of a loved one leaves a demarcation line that you use to measure ongoing holidays, birthdays, and anniversaries. In much the same way I tracked the age of my babies, this was an ongoing experience of remembering how long it had been since my husband's death. I would post on Facebook how I felt that day and was encouraged by the support of friends and family. Still, I was alone in making the decisions of how to move forward.

You can feel overwhelmed with loneliness as you face the first time you eat out alone, your first time to go to church without him/her, etc. These days can be difficult and you may just want to stay in bed with a pillow over your head. Instead, have a plan of how you will celebrate the memories and honor your loved one. Enlist the cooperation of those around you to keep you company if needed or to understand your thinking.

As you work through the first set of holidays, be wary of fulfilling the expectations of others, especially if they have no personal history of loss. Remove the pressure of fulfilling their assumptions of how you should be responding. Instead, listen to your heart. Cling to the hope that one day you will feel better. It will come when you are ready. It was somewhere during the second year that I stopped measuring time by the anniversary of my husband's death. It was a gradual shift, and it was not until later that I realized I was no longer measuring each month by this standard. I was letting go a little at a time in my own way and at my own pace.

Special days are hard anyway, so stop pretending that everything is the same. Honor the memory of your loved one by talking about how they celebrated the special day. Ride any waves of sorrow that you may feel and give others permission to do the same. My husband always gave me flowers on our wedding anniversary. Last year my kids took me out to eat and had a bouquet of flowers waiting at the table when we got to the restaurant. It was a special way of celebrating our tradition while creating a new one.

## JOIN A SUPPORT GROUP

Support groups can be a valuable resource once the shock of the death wears off. Join a support group through your church or your funeral home where you can meet others who are handling similar grief. If you're feeling alone in dealing with your grief, it can be helpful to be around others who are experiencing the same pain. Grief Share is an excellent grief recovery support group (http://www.griefshare.org). I thoroughly enjoyed the workbook and the exercises that caused me to look at my feelings.

Death and the grief that follows in its wake can be overwhelming. You may want to run and hide from everyone. Resist that temptation and join others who are walking down the same path. These support groups are not about wallowing in self-pity, but rather they are about facing the pain before moving forward.

If you have the resources to do so, go see a counselor who specializes in grief. Many times, companies have Employee Assistance Programs (EAP) in which they pay for specialized counseling for their employees who are facing a life-altering crisis.

## FACE REGRETS

One of the hardest parts about a death is the final separation and inability to speak with the loved one, especially if harsh words had been spoken. When there are unresolved issues and regrets, it can be very helpful to write a letter to your loved one expressing exactly how you're feeling. Just working through the issue and putting words around it can be a great help. However, in order to move forward with the grieving process, it is important to process what you believe about each situation. As regrets surface, write each one down so you can work through the feelings and beliefs.

In a journal or with a trusted friend, think through and process the following questions:

1. What are you feeling when you think about this memory?
2. What do you picture in your mind when you think about that?
3. Do you see the Lord anywhere in that memory?
4. If not, ask Him, "Where are You?" And then wait for something to come to mind.
5. Ask Him, "Lord, what do You want me to know about this?"

## TAKE CARE OF YOURSELF

Grief takes its toll on your body. In the days immediately after my husband died, I couldn't eat anything because my stomach was in knots. Others turn to food for comfort and may tend to overeat. In the beginning, listen to your body. As time progresses, establish new routines to eat healthy food, exercise regularly, and get plenty of rest. It is not selfish to put your needs first.

When you're in pain, it may be difficult to recognize your own needs. Be gentle with yourself as you adjust to the 'new normal.' If you prefer some time alone, communicate that to others. If you need to be around people so you don't have to be alone, then ask others to be with you.

When a loved one dies, particularly a spouse, it's important to focus on growth areas as you prepare to move forward without your loved one. You are still the same person as when they were alive, so your level of confidence and independence will carry over. Regardless, there will be an adjustment in your identity.

Take an inventory of your strengths and areas where you need to grow. Make a list of places you want to visit, people you want to meet, and experiences you long to have. Find ways to visit these places. Start making long-term plans and enjoy them. Explore places you've always wanted to go. For me, it was going to my 50th state. Two years after Bill's death, I took my father on an Alaskan cruise. We had a wonderful time and celebrated how much my mother and Bill would have enjoyed the experience. There is great peace in knowing that, as beautiful as our surroundings were, they are enjoying a more amazing experience in the presence of the Lord.

Plan something to celebrate every day. It's important to be able to look forward to something when you wake up. The possibilities are endless and don't have to be big or expensive. It can be lunch with a friend, watching a movie, borrowing a book, or starting a class to learn a new skill. Find what will work for you and your interests.

## PRAYER

Lord, I trust You in this mourning process and thank You that I don't have to be like anyone else because I am unique. You will not abandon me even as my body is wracked with sobs. I find great comfort in knowing that You are very aware of my sorrow. You collect my tears and record each one in Your book (Psalm 56:8 NLT).

Right now, I feel like I'm starting on an unending journey where the road ahead seems to lead me into complete darkness. I am looking to You so that I will not be shaken. You will protect me as I run to You for safety. You will set me on the path to life. You are always with me, even when I might not sense Your presence, and You will fill me with joy once again. I want to know the pleasures that are to be found forever at Your right hand (Psalm 16:8-11).

Even though I'm afraid that I may not make it through the days ahead, I know that You will answer me as I seek You. You will deliver me from all my fears (Psalm 34:4). Give me eyes to see the hope rays that will soon find their way from behind the dark clouds that cover me right now. Thank You for opening my eyes to Your light (Psalms 36:9 MSG). I am trusting You for blessing and favor in the days ahead. I am thankful that You are aware of the expressions on my face. You see my sadness and despair. I am so thankful that You truly care for me and we can walk this path together. Having You in my life fills me with hope because You are kind and gracious to me (Numbers 6:24-26).

In Jesus' name. Amen.

## HOPE EXPRESSIONS

*Seek the Lord and His strength; seek His face evermore!*
*Psalm 105:4 NKJV*

# Chasing Rainbows

Many friends and family who had gone through the loss of loved ones advised me to go early to the funeral home for the viewing since it can be one of the hardest parts of saying goodbye. Grief gripped my heart the night before as I faced death's finality. I worried that Bill's mouth would be open because the Muscular Dystrophy had atrophied the muscles in his face. He could no longer smile or even close his mouth.

I prayed all the way to the funeral home.

I walked into the empty room and walked over to the coffin. My eyes went immediately to his mouth and I was pleased to see they had managed to keep it closed. He was wearing his favorite Hawaiian shirt.

"Well, honey, I guess this is goodbye," I said through my tears.

That's when I felt the Holy Spirit speak to my heart, "Why are you talking to him? He's not here, but I am."

At that moment, I felt a palpable presence of the Lord in the room. For the next hour, I walked around the room and prayed for those who would be coming. I would circle back around to look at my husband's worn out body. He had held onto faith in the midst of incredible physical challenges. He had run a good race and finished strong.

I felt like a comforter had wrapped around my cold heart. I had worried about this day for a long time. I had feared that I would not be able to go on without my husband. The previous two and a half years of caring for him had been difficult. They were uncertain times filled with hard spots, yet the Lord was with us every step of the way. I was starting on a new chapter of my life. I knew it would be a hard one, but it would be good.

Soon family and friends began filing into a room filled with the presence of the Lord. I felt overwhelming peace. I was able to hug and thank every single person for coming. I just wished that Bill could have seen the outpouring of love at that moment. There were those who refused to come in where Bill's body lay, so I went to them.

After all our guests left, our family gathered around the coffin. Our grandsons followed our example and stood there without fear or trepidation. One of the twins reached out and touched the stubborn patch of hair on his Papa's forehead.

"Sweetie, this was Papa's earth suit. He's no longer here, and I know you will miss him," I said as I hugged him. He leaned into me and sighed deeply. My prayers were answered. We felt peace.

Below is a treasured keepsake my son-in-love, Jacob, wrote that day:

*The morning that we heard the news about Dad's passing, I was in a daze, but what I remember most was how ordinary, how normal the day felt. As Levi (our son) and I drove from our house to Nona and Papa's house, traffic was still moving. The sun was out. People went about their business. I was angry and frustrated that it seemed the world did not acknowledge that someone so special was no longer with us.*

*As we approached the house, the storm began to move in and the clouds blocked the sun. About an hour or so after being inside the house, I looked outside. I found that while I wept, raindrops were falling from the sky. The rain continued from that moment until the car ride from the funeral home to Nona and Papa's house today. As I was driving, I called Megan to let her know that a rainbow filled the sky. It was bold and beautiful. From my vantage point, the crest of the arch was directly above their house. Three days after the clouds filled the sky, the sun had broken through to send a message.*

*While the world continued on that day, as it should, God wanted us to know that He recognized our family had lost a significant person. Our hearts were weeping, as the skies did that day. He knows and understands our sorrow for no longer being able to share our lives with Papa. However, he is home. He is no longer bound by the condition he had. He's free! I take comfort in knowing that, literally, the seasons changed the day he passed. If ever there was a sign from God—that is it.*

In the time since my husband's death, I have given myself permission to feel my emotions fully and to mourn completely. This process can be messy and at times even a little scary. Life can never be the same as it was before Bill's death. I have many memories, yet they can be as fleeting as a rainbow in the sky. I miss Bill so much that at times it's like an ache. I have a deep longing to speak to him and feel him squeeze my hand one more time.

A few weeks later, it was raining when I picked up my grandsons from school. Right after the downpour of rain, the sun broke through the clouds.

"It's perfect weather for hope rays," I told them. "Everyone look up to see when they break through the clouds."

Everyone started looking up with expectation of what was coming next. That's the reality of the expectation of hope. When the clouds come and the rain falls, it's easy to bury ourselves in our activities to the point of feeling numb. The problem with avoiding pain is that the numbing process is not selective. If you stop feeling the bad feelings, you will also stop feeling the good ones. You may not shed tears, but you will not experience the joy in little things.

"Look, Nona! It's a rainbow," said one of the boys. And there it was—a perfect rainbow just like the ones we saw the day we said goodbye to Papa's earth suit. It only lasted for a few seconds, but we felt happy. I rushed home to get my camera so I could get a picture. By the time we got there, the rainbow had vanished. What remained were memories of a wonderful man who is now in the presence of God, enjoying the perpetual rainbow that doesn't fade.

# Hope Tools

## FIND JOY EVERY MORNING

Psalm 30:5 (NKJV) says, "Weeping may endure for a night, but joy comes in the morning." I took this quite literally to mean that I did not have to endure a long season of mourning that one day would miraculously lift. Instead, I gave myself permission to cry every night with great hope that I would experience joy the next morning. I would ride the wave of sorrow upon awakening, and then I would ask the Lord to carry that sorrow and give me purpose. As I embraced my pain, it was as if I were leaning into the Lord. A deep sense of peace would replace my feelings of despair and sorrow. This miracle happened every day. I could face the day with strength and joy.

Don't be afraid to lose control of your emotions. In the beginning, it may feel like you are on the edge of a dark precipice and jumping in brings a sense of panic. Although you can stop the flow of tears by numbing the pain instead of processing it, the problem with that approach is that the pain does not go away. Rather, it finds expression in other forms, usually in ways that can destroy your relationships. I spoke recently with a widow who felt completely numb. She believed that it was safer to stay in a place where she didn't feel anything. Fortunately, she followed my advice to see a counselor and is now dealing with her feelings in a much healthier way. While it is still difficult, she is processing the pain and moving forward.

Hope clings to the belief that God will somehow bring good from unspeakable tragedy. Although you may never fully understand while on this earth, you can trust that God is aware of your sorrow and is there to help you move toward life and light. Depending on the circumstances of the death, you may feel guilt and regrets that are hard to release. You may also be held captive by the fear that your loved one will be forgotten. These emotions can make you feel like you are being held under water. In these times of suffering, you may not know how to pray or even have words to express the deep pain. This is when the Holy Spirit comes, as it says in Romans 8:26, 28 (MSG), "God's spirit is right alongside helping us along. If we don't know how or what to pray, it doesn't matter. He does our praying in and for us, making prayer out of our wordless sighs, our aching groans . . . That's why we can be so sure that every detail in our lives of love for God is worked into something good."

First Peter 5:7 (NLT) tells you to "give all your worries and cares to God, for he cares about you."

So, face exactly what you are feeling. Emotions are simply revealing what is underneath. They are not good or bad—they are simply there. Stop judging yourself or allowing others to pressure you in this area. As you embrace your emotions, you will begin to come to grips with the reality of the separation from your loved one. You did not choose this path, and you may feel angry with God. If so, admit that to Him. Try to express to God exactly what you are feeling. Be open and honest with Him, and then ask Him what He wants to show you in this time. Resist the trap of self-pity. It's a subtle matter of perspective. Embrace your grief without making it your identity. Enjoy a good cry with cleansing tears. Then ask the Lord to carry your sadness. He will be faithful to take all you are willing to release. While you are sad and miss your loved one, it's okay to feel joy and to laugh. Give yourself permission to laugh again. That may be the greatest honor you can give your loved one.

## RELEASE PERSONAL GRIEF EXPECTATIONS

I was swimming at the health club a few weeks after Bill's death. A woman I had met a few times knew that I was my husband's caregiver. When she found out that he had died, she said, "Well, honey, you are in denial. I can tell the stage that someone is in when they are going through the grieving process. I bet your next one will be anger."

What I've learned about my grief journey is that that you cannot plan, organize, or segment the grief process. There are no quick shortcuts that will get you to the other side of the valley of the shadow of death. Grieving can be messy, unorganized, scattered, and heart-wrenching.

I was able to feel the pain and begin moving forward once I let go of what I thought grief was supposed to look like. In the same way, you have your own journey to take through this dark valley. No formulas or easy fixes will get you to the other side of your grief. But you can get there. Keep taking steps in the right direction with confidence that you will come out on the other side with greater personal strength and compassion for others who are walking on a similar path.

Feel free to explore your feelings and take as long as you need. Just keep in mind that it can be easy to get stuck in your grief. When you are tempted to give up, ask for help.

In the first few weeks immediately after my husband died, I wanted the pain to go away. It was so intense that at times it seemed unbearable. I was tempted to numb the emotions by getting busy and pushing it aside. Thankfully, I understood that if I allowed myself to feel this sadness fully, I could receive real peace and even joy by taking it to the Lord. Much like gathering all the items you need to pack for a trip, I would look all around inside my heart and gather the sadness from every corner. When I was willing to give it to the Lord, He would carry it for me. It was a gradual process of feeling the sadness, asking the Lord to carry it, releasing it to Him, and moving forward with my day. Later, when I felt it once again, I could start the process over without feeling any condemnation. This was not a one-time event that would eradicate all pain. It was instead the process of putting all of my burdens on Him and partnering with the One who is a patient friend of grief (Isaiah 53:3 VOICE).

## REST

The death of someone you love hits you right in the face. It can shake everything you believe in and leave you asking why. After the flurry of activities dies down and everyone returns to their lives, you have to start picking up the pieces in an attempt to get back to 'normal.' It can feel overwhelming.

What can you do when your body is so tired you can't take another step but your mind won't stop racing? There can be many reasons why it is so hard to get true rest. In the following paragraphs are four tips for what you can do when you need to rest.

## RELAX

Lie down on your bed or on a mat on the floor. Take a deep breath and let your muscles relax. Focus on relaxing one group of muscles at a time. Start with your toes and go all the way up to your head. Feel the weight of each muscle group before moving to the next. When you are finished, scan your entire body for any muscle groups that are not fully relaxed. Be intentional about relaxing these muscles. One of the best ways to use this technique is to make a recording where you give yourself these instructions. Often, I am asleep before I get to end of the recording.

## EXHALE AND INHALE DEEPLY

You cannot control death. Perhaps your loved one died despite all your efforts to care for them or maybe it was unexpected and shocking. One thing that you can control completely is the sequence of deep breathing. Deep breathing causes your body to get into alignment and fully relax. Imagine you are floating on a warm, gentle ocean. Imagine you are floating on your back. Inhale deeply when you rise on the swells of the gentle waves and exhale as you sink down into the waves. Lean back and let the water of God's grace carry you. Your Heavenly Father wants you to know that He is placing His powerful hands underneath you so you will not drown in the sea of grief.

## SET A BEDTIME ROUTINE

If you have a hard time falling asleep at night, set a consistent time to go to sleep. Choose a time when you feel tired so you don't toss and turn. Turn off all electronic devices at least one hour before you want to fall asleep. Be careful to make your bedroom a sanctuary for rest and relaxation. Straighten up and put away the clutter. Light a scented candle that has a relaxing fragrance, such as lavender. If you wake up during the night, go ahead and get up. Make yourself a cup of chamomile tea. Get out your journal and write about your feelings. My favorite activity during this time was to jot down the stories I would share in this book. Focus your time on prayer for your family and friends. Experiment until you can find the relaxing bedtime rituals that work best for you.

## PRAY THE WORD

There are certain Psalms and passages of lament that will allow you to put words to your feelings. As you read the Bible, highlight the scriptures that speak most to you. Memorize them and let them be a comfort. It is also powerful to use the words in these passages in your own prayers.

The prayers at the end of each chapter in this book are examples of praying the Word of God. This may be a new concept for you or one you have not used in a while. I encourage you to take your favorite verse and make it personal. Insert your name or the names of those you love. Write them in your journal. Read them aloud. As you do, your faith will soar. These prayers are powerful because they tap into the faith that comes from hearing the Word of God (Romans 10:17). Here's an example for those who might have trouble sleeping:

*I'm so tired right now, Lord, because I've been having a hard time sleeping alone since Bill died. I know You are always with me because You promised me that Your presence would always go with me wherever I go. I thank You for that reassurance of this promise. Even when my body is exhausted and wants to stop, my mind keeps racing about the uncertainties of the future. I receive this promise that You will give me rest (Exodus 33:14). As it says in Matthew 11:28 – 30 (NKJV), I come now to You because I am very tired. The heaviness of my grief is overwhelming me, especially when I try to go to sleep. You tell me I will find rest if I come to You. You also tell me that we can carry this together just as two oxen put on the same yoke in order to pull heavy burdens. Teach me how to deal with the heavy burden of grief that I feel right now. Thank You for being gentle and humble in heart. Please carry the sadness for me so that I can rest tonight.*

I find comfort in the familiarity of these passages in the King James Version because as a little girl I memorized hundreds of verses. Feel free to look up the scriptures in paraphrased versions such as The Message (MSG) or The Voice. You will see that as you personalize each verse it will be exactly what you need right now. There is no right way to do this, but rather allow the Holy Spirit freedom to make the scriptures alive in a way that meets your needs. Look at this example for inspiration:

Exodus 33:14 (VOICE), "My presence will travel with you, and I will give you rest."

Matthew 11:28-30 (MSG), "Are you tired? Worn out? Burned out on religion? Come to me. Get away with me and you'll recover your life. I'll show you how to take a real rest. Walk with me and work with me—watch how I do it. Learn the unforced rhythms of grace. I won't lay anything heavy or ill-fitting on you. Keep company with me and you'll learn to live freely and lightly."

*Lord, I feel like I've been on an endless journey of grief where I know I need to sleep, but I just can't rest. You promised that You would go with me as I travel down this difficult road. Thank You for Your presence and Your peace. Thank You for the promise that I will find rest in You. You tell me to come to You when I'm tired, worn out, and burned out. So I am coming to You now because I want to recover my life. Sometimes it feels like my life is over, but You tell me that You will teach me how to recover the joy of living. Lord, please show me how to fully rest. I slow down my thinking and ask that You teach me the rhythm of Your grace. I trust You that, while this grief feels heavy right now, You are in the process of teaching me how to live freely and lightly. Thank You that I will learn this as I hang out with You.*

Personalizing the Word of God for your situation is an effective way to quickly shift your thought patterns from what seems impossible to what God can do as you trust in Him. He will keep His promises. David expressed exactly what he was feeling in the Psalms. He cried out to God for the destruction of his enemies, forgiveness when he sinned, safety when he was running from Saul, and many more. Pick up your favorite Psalm and personalize it for your current situation.

## PRAYER

Dear Lord, thank You for rainbows. The first one You ever put in the sky was the promise to restore what had been lost during a time of devastation and loss. I am grateful for the reminder that You are committed to restoring my heart. I love how You continually show Your presence in small ways when I most need to be reminded that I am not alone.

I am thankful that You can do above and beyond what I can ask (or even think) through Your incredible power at work in my life and the lives of those I love (Ephesians 3:20-21). I am asking for peace as I process this new season in my life. I seek You and Your strength. I am thankful that You will meet me as I seek Your presence (Psalm 105:4).

When I find that I can't sleep, I know that my body can rest secure as I seek Your joy and speak praise to Your name (Psalm 16:9). I choose to sing songs of joy even when my heart is troubled and I am afraid. I will remember You as I go to bed. I will meditate on all Your blessings when I wake up in the middle of the night. You have always been there to help me. I am embraced in the shadow of Your wings (Psalm 63:5-6).

Thank You for reminding me that _____ (name of loved one) is truly experiencing Your glory as she/he worships You in Heaven. While we only see glimpses of rainbows here on earth, we know that one day we also will be in Your presence where the rainbows never fade. Then we will experience all that You have for us for eternity. Grant us the wisdom and grace to walk in Your ways every minute of every day that we have here on Earth as we remember the promise of the glory of Your presence.

In Jesus' name. Amen.

## HOPE EXPRESSIONS

*Like the appearance of a rainbow in the clouds on a rainy day, so was the radiance around him. This was the appearance of the likeness of the glory of the LORD.*
*Ezekiel 1:28*

# Embracing Lament

The morning after my husband died, I woke up with sobs racking my body. They were so intense that I walked outside so I would not wake up my son who still lived with me at the time. I sat on the steps on the front porch and gave vent to the intense sorrow that welled up from the very core of my being. My overwhelming emotions literally took my breath away. My heart physically hurt and my sides ached. I don't know how long I wept. I do know that it was dark when I went out and I saw the sunrise. This became a pattern for the following months. I gave myself permission to fully embrace the tears and everything I was feeling. At times, I felt like I was going to drown in an ocean of grief. That's when I decided to study what the Bible has to say about suffering.

The Sunday school lessons I heard as a child were as flat as the two-dimensional coloring sheet of a man sitting on the ground with sores all over his body. Job was portrayed as a man who lacked faith because he says in Job 3:25 that what he feared came upon him. After Bill's death, I decided to reread this small book in the Old Testament. What I discovered was a multi-dimensional panorama of the struggles and triumphs of a man who had it all and then lost it all. In the painful process of embracing lament, Job found that his greatest treasure was an open relationship with God.

The Bible is very real and holds nothing back when talking about Job's trials. His life was exposed in heart-wrenching detail. The story starts with a conversation between God and the accuser who challenges Job's untested faith. In other words, anyone can be faithful to God when everything is going great. And right there is the problem with Job's suffering. He didn't deserve any of it. He was an upright man who sought to do everything God's way. Then suddenly, the bottom drops out of his perfect world. He literally lost everything—his livelihood, his possessions, his family, and finally, his health.

Job managed to keep his composure as he received the first three messages that came one right on top of the other. Just as soon as one messenger finished, another one showed up with the bad news of business losses and the death of his workers. Then the message comes that all of his children died when a tornado from the desert struck the house where they were having a party. At that point, Job does something very significant. He falls on to the ground and worships (Job 1:20). In the next verse, we hear familiar words: "Naked I came from my mother's womb, naked I'll return to the womb of the earth. God gives, God takes. God's name be ever blessed" (Job 1:21 MSG).

The choice to bless the name of the Lord in the midst of extreme suffering becomes the foundation of Job's hope. He is not denying his pain but rather seeking the presence of God in the midst of it all. His mourning opens the door to true worship even when he didn't understand the reasons why he was suffering. What we read in the remainder of his story rests on this pursuit of God's presence. This becomes Job's true north on the compass as he further navigates through the loss of health and the advice of his friends.

One of the hardest issues for someone reeling from a major loss can be the way that those closest to us provide superficial answers. Those who have been untested can often be quick to give their advice. It leaves you cold.

Job's friends came to comfort him. To their credit, they sat in silence for a long time, but when they started talking, they were not helpful. They believed that the only reason for his suffering was that he had done something wrong. Their beliefs mirror many today who feel they have to find the reason why tragedy strikes someone who is serving God. Is it a hidden sin or lack of faith? These so-called friends droned on and on until Job could take it no more. He finally kicked them out.

At that point, it's as if Job gets in the ring with God. Everyone around him told him to throw in the towel. He should just give up. But he held his ground and confronted God with his doubts and questions. No matter what anyone else said, Job determined to remain honest and that is where he finally heard from God. It's okay to ask God the hard questions with an honest heart and to cry out in our pain. The hope in Job's mourning comes from a transparent personal relationship with God. He had heard about God, but now he is experiencing Him in a real way. Job declares in Job 42:5, "My ears had heard of you but now my eyes have seen you."

In many ways, Bill was like Job. Here was a man who loved God more than anything, yet suffered every day without complaining. He was a great man who served God with all of his heart. So why did God let him suffer so much and ultimately let him die when he had so much to offer? I grappled with these questions during his last two and a half years and after his death. Peace can be elusive as you pick up the pieces of your life and try to return to 'normal' after the death of a loved one. Just one month earlier, my training session had ended abruptly with the call about my husband's death during the night. Now it was time to return and conduct the training. While I was looking forward to getting back to a routine, part of me dreaded stepping back into that classroom.

When the participants started arriving, I realized that many of them had been praying for me. I got many hugs and condolences. The training sessions went well and I was grateful for the positive response to the material I was presenting. Most of all, I was thankful to be surrounded by caring people.

That evening I returned to the empty classroom to finish some paperwork. I closed the door, turned on the worship music, and began to thank the Lord for all He had done. In that moment, I began to experience peace that went far beyond what I could manufacture in my mind. This was more than a mental assent to the fact that Bill is now in a 'better place.'

The final test came when "Blessed Be the Name" started playing—the worship song that had ministered to me the day I got the news. Many might have thought I had totally lost my mind if they could have seen me. I started singing loudly, waving my hands and emphasizing the truth contained in its lyrics. "He gives and takes away, my heart will choose to say, Lord, blessed be your name!"

Peace is much more than the absence of conflict. Peace is an inner calm that defies explanation. It is a place of rest that comes from an inner reservoir of hope—a hope that tells you that everything is going to be okay. This is confidence born from faith that I don't have to understand everything right now. I can just rest in knowing that I can ask for what I need moment by moment. As I thank Him for what He is doing in my life, I will have the strength to make it through another day. For now that's enough. I am grateful for peace that is bigger than what I can come up with or can even understand. This peace guards my heart and mind.

What do you do when you feel like you are in over your head? What do you do when darkness is closing in? It's a scary and lonely place. Seek refuge in God when you feel overwhelmed by the circumstances that you cannot control. It's the same principle as floating on water. It makes no sense that if you relax the water will support your weight. In the same way, as you release your grip and allow God to carry your anger, anxiety, and fear, you will find peace.

# *Hope Tools*

## BE HONEST WITH GOD

As you start on this grief journey, look for someone who is willing to listen without judging or trying to solve your issues. If you don't have anyone to talk to, write in your journal. The most important thing is to be completely honest with what you are feeling. The circumstances of the death of your loved one may be very different from what I have described. It may be that you need to find ways to redeem the senseless tragedy of a suicide or drug overdose. This can be difficult when you feel regret and pain over the circumstances.

Memories may be painful bridges to the past. Every bridge is significant, whether it is a good memory or a painful one. Take time to face your fears and anxieties. Identify your emotions and see if a memory comes to mind where you have felt that way before. Feel the pain of the memory and then ask for God's perspective right there. He longs to give you hope and truth.

Sometimes your perspective of God can get skewed as you look at the circumstances surrounding the death of your loved one. You may feel angry with God because of what happened. God is able to handle your anger. He knows that it's in your heart anyway. Anger is an honest emotion that only becomes wrong when you hang on to it and it turns into bitterness. Be honest with God about your feelings and then be willing to hear His response.

## GET GOD'S PERSPECTIVE

Many of us are divided on where we stand regarding the subject of suffering. In fact, we hear few sermons on this topic despite the fact that every single person in the Bible had their share of hard times. For this reason, it's very important to step back and look at our grief from God's point of view and invite Him in to share our pain and sorrow. Here are steps to accomplish this in your life:

- Express all your feelings. Don't hold anything back. God knows what's in your heart so there is no reason to pretend. You might find it easier to write down exactly what is going through your mind.

- Be sure to address any anger issues. I was always taught that it was wrong to be angry, and so I found it difficult to let God know I was angry. Once I told Him openly how angry I felt for Bill's illness, I was able to release the burden of carrying that emotional baggage. You might be angry at the person who died or those around who didn't carry their weight during difficult times.

- Identify who you are angry with and why you are angry with them. Anger is a protective emotion. The reason people hold on to anger is because they believe it is helping them in some way. Therefore, in order to replace the anger with peace, examine your motives carefully. What is the anger doing for you? If you weren't angry at _____, what do you believe would happen?

- Now, ask the Lord if what you are believing about the anger is true. Listen for His perspective, and let the Lord replace the anger with His truth and peace. You can live with perfect peace as you begin to think like He does. In 2 Thessalonians 3:16 (VOICE), we read, "And now, dear friends, may the Lord of peace Himself grace you with peace always and in everything. May the Lord be present with all of you." Inviting the Lord into every situation and feeling His presence brings peace.

## IDENTIFY YOUR LOSSES

Relationships are complex. Someone who was a part of your everyday life is no longer there. That leaves a hole with losses on many different levels. As you embrace the sorrow that you feel, you can find true comfort from the Lord. You can also let those around you know what you need. Make a list or a mind-map of your losses. A mind-map is a good tool for this exercise because it releases your creative juices in areas that you might not otherwise think. This list will help you get started: companion, lover, cheerleader, spouse, balance, faith builder, mechanic, cuddler, cook, walking companion, etc.

Recently I experienced some hard times financially. I knew that the Lord was going to supply because He had always done so in the past. After completing my mind-map, I realized that what I most missed at this specific time was Bill squeezing my hand in reassurance and faith that we would make it through this even as we had so many times before. Although he was unable to speak due to his breathing difficulties, his hands remained as strong as his faith. At a recent prayer group meeting, I was able to express what I was feeling. The group gathered around me to pray and hold my hand. This Hope Tool helped me to identify what I needed so I could then communicate it to others.

## REVISIT THE MEMORIAL SERVICE

Bill and I never talked at length about his wishes for his funeral. However, he did have one very specific request. "Please promise me that you won't have my funeral service at the mortuary," he said. "It's just too depressing for people. I want it to be a celebration and I want a lot of worship. That's what I will be doing. You have no idea how many times when I'm worshipping I have longed to be able to lift my arms all the way to the sky. I know that one day God will heal my shoulders. I continue to believe that it will be here on earth. But, either way, I will get the desire of my heart. I won't give you a lot more details because you'll do what you want to do anyway," he said with a wink. "Remember the good times, the beach in California, the adventures in Nicaragua and Costa Rica, the fun we had at camp, and the love we shared at Praise Unlimited."

When it was time to plan Bill's memorial service, I remembered our conversation and planned accordingly. I led worship from the piano, Sean played the guitar, and Sarah and Megan sang. I reached out to family and friends so they could share from each of the chapters in Bill's life. It certainly was not your typical funeral service. One of our friends has a video business and he recorded the service. That recording has been a treasure, not just for those who were unable to attend, but for me as well. I sobbed the first few times I watched it. Then, as I continued to watch it, I caught nuances of what the speakers shared and remembered rich experiences we had.

Keep the audio recording or a video of the funeral or memorial service in a safe place. Watch it on a monthly basis in order to get in touch with your feelings. It could be that on the day of the actual service you were numb from the shock and could not process all that you were feeling. You will receive comfort as you face your emotions. Give yourself full permission to cry, but also to laugh as you ride the waves to comfort.

## PRAYER

Sometimes I feel like the weight of grief and sorrow is going to crush me. I am so grateful that You hear my cries and listen to my prayers. When my heart grows faint and I feel overwhelmed, You lead me to a place of safety. I am so thankful that You are my refuge (Psalm 61:1-4 TLB).

There are those times I feel like my sorrow is too great even for Your healing touch. When I feel devastated with grief, You welcome me back with enormous compassion. You love me with everlasting love and show such tender care for me (Isaiah 54:7-8 MSG). I thank You that You will restore me to health physically, emotionally, and spiritually. I know that You will heal my wounds and that I will be stronger than I ever thought possible.

In Jesus' name. Amen.

## HOPE EXPRESSIONS

*The Spirit of the Sovereign Lord is on me, because the Lord has anointed me to proclaim good news to the poor. He has sent me to bind up the brokenhearted, to proclaim freedom for the captives and release from darkness for the prisoners, to proclaim the year of the Lord's favor and the day of vengeance of our God, to comfort all who mourn, and provide for those who grieve in Zion—to bestow on them a crown of beauty instead of ashes, the oil of joy instead of mourning, and a garment of praise instead of a spirit of despair. They will be called oaks of righteousness, a planting of the Lord for the display of his splendor.*

*Isaiah 61:1-3*

# Remembering Little Things

I remember Bill's last supper. I wish I had known that it would be the last time we would eat together. Most of us do not realize the impact of small events in life until we no longer have them. As the Muscular Dystrophy progressed, swallowing became increasingly difficult for Bill. In the end, he received his nutrients through a feeding tube in his stomach. But if I had realized that last supper was the last meal we would share, I would have made his favorite—meatloaf, mashed potatoes, and corn. I would have insisted that we sit at the table with all the kids and grandkids. I would have baked a German chocolate cake, his favorite dessert. We would have savored every bite and enjoyed the conversation. Instead, we ate tacos from Taco Bell.

Jesus modeled some important principles for mourning when He sat down to eat His last meal with His friends and followers. Unlike me, He knew it was the last time He would eat with them here on this earth. He tried to tell His disciples that this was a very significant meal because of the suffering that was ahead for Him and the challenges they would face. They didn't get it. This passage is very familiar and has differing religious and legalistic overtones that can keep us from grasping the deeper meaning behind His words. He actually gave us a great pattern of how to mourn because He was preparing those He loved to live without His physical presence.

As seen in Luke 22, when it was time for Passover, Jesus sent Peter and John to find the place where they would eat what has become known as 'The Last Supper.' As always, He used creative ways to select the ones who would provide the setting for this dinner party. He told them they would see a man carrying a pot of water. That struck me as odd, so I did a little research only to find that no self-respecting man in Jesus' time would carry a pitcher of water in public because that was a woman's job.

I can imagine the following conversation could have taken place as Peter and John went about their assignment.

"I sure wish the Master wouldn't leave these details to the last minute," griped Peter.

"Peter, you know it always works out just fine," said John.

"Oh, I guess you're right. Look at all these people. Jerusalem is always so crowded around this time of the year. All the rooms are probably already booked. Here's another thing: when was the last time you saw a man carrying a pitcher of water? That's a woman's job," continued the outspoken one.

"Rabbi has never been wrong before, so let's just see what happens, okay?" replied John.

"Well, I hate to admit it, but you're right. Isn't that a man with a pitcher of water?" asked Peter. "I'm going to go ask him why he decided to get the water today instead of sending one of the women to do it."

"Remember, we're just supposed to follow him," answered John.

"Oh, that's right. Hurry up. We're going to lose him. I doubt there are two guys out here with pitchers of water!" Peter exclaimed.

They did as they were told. Following the man to a two-story house, they walked in and asked the owner of the house if he had a second story room where they could celebrate the Passover. He not only had a room, but it was clean and ready for them to use that night. We get no other details about the logistics of this meal—no mention of who cooked it or anything else—yet we see that God's provision is always present when we need it. The Lord mixes up the social order to accomplish His purposes even when it seems to be at the last minute. He truly has a plan in it all.

## SMALL THINGS BECOME IMPORTANT

So often, in retrospect, we realize the importance of seemingly insignificant things. They become valuable by virtue of the fact that they are now gone. Most of us live as if we will always have what we currently have now. Only later do we realize that what we had was very special. Even though Jesus was telling them it was their last time to eat together, they didn't grasp the full impact of His words and actions until later. I can relate.

Rick Miller is one of Bill's closest friends. He's really more like a brother because their families shared the early years of their lives in small town Placentia, California. As kids, Rick and Bill played outside until sundown. They went to school together, learned how to drive together, and shared a lifetime of memories.

The last time we were visited by Rick and his wife Esther, known affectionately as Butchie, Bill gave special instructions that surprised me.

"Go take them to pick anything they want from the third shelf in my room," Bill quickly scribbled on his whiteboard.

"I just can't take anything," Butchie said tearfully as we headed down the hall to the bedroom.

"Well, you better. When I bring him back here tonight, he'll be checking," I replied with a smile.

Tears welled up in my eyes as we stood staring at an assortment of items from Bill's life-long collections. They were both visibly shaken by this request, yet I didn't want to worry about it. After they hugged Bill and said their goodbyes, I walked out to their car with them.

"I want you to know that the doctors have given Bill a good prognosis. They say his heart and lungs are strong. As long as we're careful with his swallowing, I believe we're going to have him with us for a nice long time," I reassured them.

Just like the disciples, I was too close to the situation to hear what Bill was saying. I thought I knew better. I guess I'm a lot like Peter in that way. I wonder how many times Peter mentally rewound the conversations of that evening. Like me, I'm sure he shook his head because he really didn't get it until later. I wonder if he looked back on the last meal they shared and wished that he had really understood what Jesus was saying. I take creative license in retelling the following story based on John 13.

## FEET WASHING TIME

Peter and John had been the ones who set up this meal. I wonder if they forgot to hire the servant who would wash their feet. Regardless, Jesus took the towel and bowl that the servants used to wash the dirty, smelly feet of guests. As He started washing their feet, Peter felt something well up inside him. He couldn't believe the others would let Jesus do the job of a menial servant. Someone needed to protest. He was ready with his speech when it was his turn.

"Oh no, Master. You're not going to wash my feet!" exclaimed Peter. "I need to be the one washing Your feet because You're the teacher."

Jesus looked up with love in His eyes. From that vantage point, Peter no doubt felt like Jesus could see right through him with all his faults and shortcomings, his pride and arrogance, his insecurities and struggles.

"Oh, Peter. If you don't let Me wash your feet and teach you this important lesson, you won't be able to have any part in My future plans for you," Jesus answered.

"Well, in that case, wash all of me!" Peter exclaimed.

Jesus was once again messing with Peter's preconceived notions of how things were 'supposed' to be done. Jesus took advantage of this moment to teach a valuable lesson. First, He gave instructions to find a man carrying water, and now He bends down to wash Peter's feet. These acts were intended to teach all of His followers the importance of changing the way they look at life. As He took the bowl and towel and stooped down to wash their dirty feet, He was teaching them a Kingdom principle about serving. Grieving is dirty and messy, just like their feet. Jesus was showing them that they did not have to hide their faults and shortcomings. After the cross, where He took upon Himself all their sin, they would now be able to live fully. After His resurrection, they were able to understand the words He had spoken to them at that last meal.

Jesus used an illustrated message about how to grieve when He gave instructions for His followers to break bread and drink wine in remembrance of Him. Many of us celebrate communion in our churches. We focus on these two elements that represent the sacrifice that Jesus made for us when He died on the cross. It is without a doubt a significant part of our worship to remember His death and resurrection. In the early church, it was a full meal shared with fellow believers and not just a little cup with a cracker. Sharing a meal became an intentional opportunity to open their hearts to one another to keep the memories and a legacy alive for generations to come. He knew that there would be great comfort as they sat down to share a meal and to remember His teachings and His life.

Grief is a common experience we will all share at some point in our lives. While sorrow is inevitable, we can feel the full comfort of the Lord in our time of sorrow. The act of remembering can stir up the pain of loss; ultimately, however, it is the most comforting exercise as we deliberately slow down the memory process in order to learn all that we can from the experience. Memories are precious and life lessons are priceless.

# Hope Tools

## PRESERVE MEMORIES

Time takes on a different quality in the context of a loved one's death. In ways, it can seem like yesterday because the details are vivid and seared into our memories. In other ways, it can feel like a very long time since we've heard our loved one's voice. Memories are like a kaleidoscope of impressions and lessons learned. The tapestry of our lives has the golden threads and the black ones. If it were just one color, it would be boring and bland. There are so many lessons learned and challenges that are overcome.

The memories of a lifetime become precious treasures. Make a commitment to write the memories down or make videos as you remember the milestones and seasons of a person's lifetime. One of Bill's main joys in life came from his relationships with people over the years. The sympathy cards that I received after his death highlighted the impact his life had on so many. I also went back and copied all the kind words that friends and family shared on Facebook and via email into a notebook.

## WRITE ABOUT YOUR EXPERIENCES

It's important to write whatever you are feeling in order to get the feelings out in the open. Sometimes we're not even sure what we're feeling until we start writing about it. Journals do not have to be fancy in order to be effective. They can be leather bound editions or inexpensive black and white composition books. The critical part is to write often and be completely honest. Don't put yourself under pressure if you skip a day or two. You will find, however, if you make it a habit, you will miss writing on the days you don't make time to do so.

The benefits of journaling are many. In the first place, you will be taking some time every day to reflect on your feelings that day. What I missed the most was having a daily conversation with my husband about the events of the day. Your journal can become your gentle friend that listens without judging or giving advice. Secondly, your journal will help you see how far you've come in your grief journey. You can track your progress and help others in their journey.

One way to journal is to write a blog. I started a blog called HOPEgrams (karensebastian.com/hopegrams), and I found that writing those each week helped me process what I was feeling. I kept them short and at times I didn't even publish them. Some of the content in this book came from these short writings as I processed what I was feeling at the time. Another option to keep others up-to-date is CaringBridge (CaringBridge.org). It provides a place where people can respond with their support and prayers. People really want to be supportive and this gives them a way to express that support.

Here are some suggestions to get you started:

- What do you miss most?

- What was the best part of your relationship?

- Why is it hard to keep going?

- What was the most amazing part of your loved one's life?

- What do you wish you had known about him/her?

- What details do you remember of the memorial service?

- What most touched your heart about the days immediately after your loved one's death?

- What was the last conversation you had with your loved one?

- What are other tender moments?

## CREATE A TREASURE CHEST OF MEMORIES

Find creative ways to capture memories. It can be a box with cards, pictures, and journal entries or a hard drive full of pictures and videos. The most important thing is to have a way to go back and enjoy the memories. Tell stories and laugh with others as you share the good times.

At family gatherings, ask different people what they enjoyed most about the life and contributions of the one who died. Get input from others about how they want to commemorate the anniversary of the loved one's death. Some will want to visit the cemetery or columbarium while others may want to go to a place where they shared wonderful memories.

## MAKE A LIST OF BEST TIMES/WORST TIMES

"It was the best of times, it was the worst of times," writes Charles Dickens in *A Tale of Two Cities*. This can be a T-list where you put a large T on your paper and write Best and Worst at the top. First, think of all the worst times you went through. A great suggestion here is to hand the family some 'post-it' notes and ask them to just think back on the last few months or year of your loved one's life. What were challenges the person faced? What did you face yourself? Be transparent and open with your struggles and emotions during this time. Once you have completed the list of worsts, start thinking of all the wonderful memories. Match good memories up to the worst ones. If you're using sticky notes, use a pad of a different color.

The purpose of this exercise is to expand your mind past the difficult times you've encountered in the recent past. As you change your mindset, you will discover blessings in the hard days and the benefits gleaned even in suffering.

## RETELL FUNNY STORIES

One of the last 'conversations' our oldest daughter, Elizabeth, had with her dad was via text and yelling through a window. She came to visit her dad while I was out. She forgot her key to the house, and since Bill was unable to get up at that time, she stood at the window and spoke to him loudly. He replied via his text messages on her phone. These messages are now treasures.

Just today, my daughter and I were talking about some of the corny things she remembers her dad saying. We both chuckled at how this is now so funny. As a teenager, she would roll her eyes at her dad's puns. Now she finds herself repeating the same phrases and having a little chuckle every time.

## Prayer

Lord, thank You for the gift of remembering _____'s life. In some ways, it's painful to go to these memories, yet You taught us to remember Your death and suffering. As I remember the little things about him/her that drove me crazy, I find myself smiling through the tears. I thank You for the special gift of _____. Thank You for his/her life and what he/she taught us.

Even as I remember the difficult times that we went through, I am thankful that Your grace was enough to carry us through the hard times. Thank You for helping us to remember the good moments in the darkest places. You gave us the strength to live by faith and not by sight (2 Corinthians 5:7), and you have carried us through these times as I know you're carrying me now (Isaiah 46:4).

Lord, as I remember, I feel like I have lost so much that I now have empty gaps in my heart. Please come and fill these places with Your love and peace. I receive Your grace to continue to move through this time of mourning with blessing and hope for a bright future.

In Jesus' name. Amen.

## HOPE EXPRESSIONS

*Thank [God] in everything [no matter what the circumstances may be, be thankful and give thanks], for this is the will of God for you [who are] in Christ Jesus [the Revealer and Mediator of that will].*
*1 Thessalonians 5:18 AMP*

# Cherishing Special Days

When Bill died, I wanted everything to stop. But it didn't. In fact, life went on much the same as before. Our family experienced this personally when Bill's father died. Grief overtook his mom in such a way that she wanted to give up. She wanted to die too. So we moved in with her. That was a difficult season because she was angry and depressed.

"Promise me that when it's my time to go, you will keep on living," Bill told me once while we lived with his mom in the house where he was raised.

"What do you mean? Don't talk that way," I chided him as fear gripped my heart just to think of life without him.

"I know it will be hard, but life goes on," he replied. "So promise me..."

"Okay, I will . . . but don't you even think of leaving anytime soon," I answered.

Thankfully, we had thirty more wonderful years together. We moved to Texas, and shortly after, my mother-in-love moved in with us. She lived with us for almost twelve years. During that time, we saw her shrink emotionally and physically from the weight of grief. She seemed to feel that if she fully enjoyed life she would stop showing her undying love to her husband. I promised Bill I would not do that when it was his turn.

Bill died in September, just two months before our youngest son, Sean, married his sweetheart, Sarah. Bill was determined to go to the wedding despite his physical difficulties and restrictions. We ordered a power wheel-chair, and he practiced driving it in preparation. Sarah was preparing to practice her dance around the chair. I made the reservation for the rental van that had a built-in ramp. The night before his dad died, Sean sat on his bed and discussed details of the wedding rehearsal and other future plans, excitedly telling him about the apartment they had leased just that day. They made sure that it had wheelchair access.

There was never any doubt about what Bill would want us to do with the wedding plans. Move forward.

Three days before the wedding, our kids got the news that the outdoor wedding venue needed to change because the weatherman was predicting rain. I've never been more proud of them as they responded to this challenge and embraced the last-minute changes. Up until the day of the wedding, the weather had been very warm without a cloud in the sky. As predicted, massive clouds filled the sky the day of the wedding, and there were scattered thunderstorms that morning.

With the change in venue, last minute supplies were needed. That morning I got ready and packed up the car with everything that I needed to take. I was planning to get there early just in case anything slipped through the cracks. As I left the house, I had this feeling that I was forgetting something. Sure enough, I had forgotten to take the gallons of iced tea that I had purchased the day before. Fortunately, I still had plenty of time to go to a nearby store after I dropped off my family and the other items.

"Where's the nearest store?" I asked the wedding consultant.

"You can't miss it. Go out to the main street and then turn right. It will be on the left," she replied.

I somehow missed my turn, and, before I knew it, I was heading over an overpass that took me in the wrong direction. I was feeling alone and vulnerable on this special day that was meant to be shared with my beloved husband of almost forty years. That's when I looked up and saw the 'hope rays' shining from behind the clouds. The entire sky was magnificent. It seemed that a shaft of light came from every single dark cloud.

My eyes filled with tears as I looked up to see this beautiful panorama. My heart swelled with gratitude to the Lord for His goodness and mercy. I asked Him to carry my sorrow. He reminded me that I am never alone. Could it be that the glorious 'hope rays' were just for me? I do know that the Lord was very present and shared our joyful celebration of the new life ahead for these two precious ones.

The setting was magical; their exchange of vows was amazing. Laughter resonated into the night. We shared a warm family time, but one key person missed the festivities—my husband. Yet I knew that Bill would not want us to stop creating new memories and fulfilling the plans for a hope-filled future. The future has not been written. It is filled with hope.

# *Hope Tools*

## MAKE A GRATITUDE LIST

Cultivate a thankful mindset. This can be hard to do when you are caring for someone who is very sick or when someone you love dies. It takes a shift in mindset to see all the blessings you have experienced even though you are in a hard place right now. This is learned behavior where you are constantly looking for areas of gratitude. You need to begin to practice this approach to life when all is going well. Most people who are complaining about their circumstances have lost sight of what is truly important in life.

My gratitude list changed forever as I watched my husband deal with his daily physical challenges. His legacy to our family was incredible grace in the midst of increasing weakness and impossibilities.

One hot summer afternoon, I was greeting our next-door neighbor over our backyard fence. When I asked him how he was doing, he caught himself as he was about to complain about the heat. Instead he said, "Well, it's been super hot, but I can breathe and I can swallow. So I guess I better say that I am grateful." I chuckled as I went back into our cool, air-conditioned home. I must have told him before that my gratitude list had changed. After a doctor's appointment, I was grateful for the strength God gave us both to get Bill out of the car into the wheelchair and back. Every night as I went to sleep, I would think about how grateful I was that my husband had managed to make it into bed and we had the medical devices that helped him continue to breathe.

Start writing a list of things you are grateful for since the death of your loved one. Sometimes we can get so focused on the darkness that we fail to see the points of light and blessing that surround us. The first one on my list is the realization that we have so many blessings and wonderful provision for every need. It may not come ahead of time, yet it appears just when we need it most.

The day that I got the news that Bill had moved to Heaven, my gratitude list was:

- I am grateful that Bill can now swallow, can breathe, and is running around Heaven on two strong legs.

- I am grateful that Bill's arms are lifted high in praise to His Lord and Savior.

- I am grateful that Bill is singing his praises to God at the top of his lungs.

- I am grateful that Bill's beautiful soul is no longer captive in a broken-down 'earth suit.'

- I am grateful I had the honor of caring for this wonderful man.


Gratitude shifted my focus from my pain and loneliness to Bill's gain of being with the Lord.

Here are other suggestions to help you capture the reasons you are grateful:

- Start the day with your list of the blessings for which you are grateful

- Handwrite your gratitude list

- Celebrate small victories (like making it to a doctor's appointment)

## TWEAK TRADITIONS

The first major holidays and anniversaries after the death of a loved one can be difficult. The most important thing is to listen to your feelings and stay in touch with those you love. Your loved one is no longer present, but many others are there. Celebrate and honor the most beloved traditions of the one who died. Use it as a time to capture memories and honor their purpose in life.

When it comes to major holidays such as Thanksgiving and Christmas, it's important to have a discussion with the family in order to find out what's important to them. If there is a major part that was more what your loved one wanted to do, then realize that you don't have to keep everything the same. In fact, be open to starting new traditions and keep what is meaningful to your family. Create new memories to augment the old. It's not a subtraction, but rather an addition and even multiplication of the legacy of a life well lived.

## SEEK LIFE-GIVING RELATIONSHIPS

One of the amazing things about friendships is that they can evolve over time. For example, if your spouse recently died, you may find that the married couples you hung out with no longer seek you out for the weekend fun events you used to share. Or, they might invite you, but you now feel like the 'third wheel.'

Trust that you bring value to relationships as an individual. Get out of your comfort zone and seek out people who bring you joy. Sometimes it is easier to talk about your loss to people who are not grieving with you. You can make connections to people who can share the joy of the Lord with you and can minister life in the midst of the pain. Keep in mind that you will probably need to initiate the activities that will bring you in contact with new people.

## Look Up—Especially on Cloudy Days

A grief journey after the death of a loved one can seem like a long, dark tunnel. At times, it may feel like you are never going to feel whole again. When emotional darkness closes in and threatens to engulf you, it is critical to look up. Some days, like the one described in this chapter, I felt so alone and was afraid others would see my sadness. Hope abounds when we make mistakes, experience delays, and wonder why we are driving away from something instead of toward the place we are supposed to be. Hope tells me that when this happens I need to look up.

Cloudy days = Hope Rays. That seems to have been the formula for me during difficult times. As I look back over the panorama of my husband's illness, it seems like hope rays appeared every single time that I most needed them. A few times, I would look up at the sky to see hope rays and think, "I really don't need these today. Thank You, Lord, for Your comfort and reminders of Your love." Before the hope rays dissipated, I would always discover who needed them that day. I found that I was able to feel a sense of joy along with the sadness.

## PRAYER

I approach special days with trepidation because what was once a celebration is now a source of pain. God, grant me Your peace, so I can look forward to _____ (fill in birthday, anniversary, or holiday). I am missing _____ more than ever. Give me an eternal perspective in order to see that You are present in all celebrations as You watch over our lives. Thank You for being mindful of our coming and going throughout our lives and for all eternity (Psalm 121:7-8).

Lord, thank You for reminding me that I need to keep in mind the number of my own days. Keep me focused on love and wisdom as we celebrate special days to remember _____. Thank You for releasing me to feel what I need to feel during this time of grief while giving myself permission to laugh again.

I relinquish my expectations of what these special days will be and thank You for allowing my tears and my sorrow to be a bridge to Your presence in my life. Give me strength and desire to enjoy the blessings of life. You say that You are very close to those who feel like their heart is broken. That would be me right now, yet I know that one day I will see it all clearly and for now that's enough (1 Corinthians 13:12).

In Jesus' name. Amen.

## HOPE EXPRESSIONS

*Teach us to number our days, that we may gain a heart of wisdom.*
*Psalm 90:12 NKJV*

# Honoring a Legacy

Four months after my husband's death, I stood before several hundred pastors and their spouses in Costa Rica to share our family's experience of honoring Bill. My throat tightened as I tried to hold back the tears that threatened to run down my face. My biggest fear was that I would lose my composure and start sobbing uncontrollably. I prayed a quick prayer asking for guidance on how to share what the practice of honoring had done for our family and for my husband.

"A few months ago my husband moved to Heaven—without my permission I might add," I started. A few chuckles rippled through the audience.

"Bill was a humble man with one burning desire—to fulfill God's will in his life. He truly loved the Lord, his family, and all who looked to him for spiritual leadership. He was heartbroken when he had to resign as a full-time pastor because of muscle weakness. His legacy of love continued as he reached out and encouraged others. Despite physical issues, he never stopped being who he was created to be and actually became stronger spiritually," I shared.

I went on to explain that to honor is to show respect and express what we value in others. A few years ago, we started a birthday family tradition. Starting with the youngest member of the family, each person would share what he or she appreciated and valued most about the person celebrating a birthday. It was hard when we first started. It seemed awkward and a little uncomfortable, especially for the recipient. Over time, this has become the most anticipated part of our birthday celebrations. I love to see the response from my grandchildren to these words of affirmation and encouragement.

Most people only express gratitude for what others do for them. We seldom stop to let them know that we appreciate the innate qualities that make them unique and special. Due to my husband's disability, he progressively got weaker and, in the final months of his life, needed more and more care. When it was time to celebrate his last birthday, we had learned how to honor the outstanding character qualities he showed despite his physical weakness and inability to speak. He truly lived Romans 12:10 (NKJV), that says, "Be kindly affectionate to one another with brotherly love, in honor giving preference to one another."

"Please raise your hand if recently someone honored you by telling you what they admire most about your character," I told the group of ministers that sat before me. Only two or three raised their hands. Seldom, if ever, do we give the gift of honor to others unless it is part of the eulogy at a memorial service. The death of our loved one crystalizes our focus as it forces us to face why we will miss someone. We zero in on those qualities we most appreciate and love. The tragedy is that, in many cases, the person never knew how we felt while they were alive.

As I looked into the faces of those gathered there, I could see that this explanation of honor touched many. When I finished speaking, I invited the couples to take a few minutes to write down the qualities they honored in their spouses. Those who were single found someone they knew well and did the same thing. Then they sat and told each other what they had written. Tears flowed. I heard later about restored relationships in marriages. Several who were discouraged to the point of quitting the ministry found renewed purpose to continue to serve.

Each one of us will leave a heritage by how we treated others, the environment we fostered, and the blessings we passed on. I am so grateful that our family created a culture of honor that facilitated the expression of sincere appreciation for Bill's extraordinary heart and godly character. I love that we learned to honor him during his lifetime rather than waiting to share the legacy of a lifetime at a memorial service. For some, however, those missed opportunities add to the pain they feel during the grief journey. It's never too late to honor someone, and in fact, honoring the legacy of your loved one aids in healing those most painful places in your heart.

Perhaps you had a difficult and tumultuous relationship with this person. Your last conversation may have been filled with angry, stinging words. If this happened to you, you may be stuck in a loop of tormenting memories that steal your peace. It is important to seek help to break this negative cycle. Counseling and freedom ministry are two helpful options so you can bring your feelings out in the open. Once you have faced your pain openly, ask God for His perspective and listen carefully to His words of comfort. He promises to give you peace if you focus on what He has to say.

It is possible to move forward in honoring the significance of a person's life despite the circumstances of their death. In this life, you may never understand why and, sometimes, even what happened. Resist the extremes of either putting the person on a pedestal as someone who could do no wrong or making them out to be the villain. Instead, allow their story and even their mistakes to be a warning to others. For example, some parents of children who have died have set up foundations to help find a cure or even campaigned for changing a law that might prevent the same tragedy in the lives of others. If you were estranged from your loved one in the end, seek out their friends to talk about their heart and discover their passions.

You need God's strength as you continue in this grief journey to seek out the best ways to honor the legacy of the one who died. Your journey is unique and special. The strength of your hope is not found in your own capacity and understanding but in relying on the Lord. This level of hope centers you in a way that settles restlessness and confusion. You can find peace in Him.

# *Hope Tools*

## SHARE THE LEGACY

A legacy grows as you remember and honor what was important to the person who died. As you share the memories of their motivation and actions in life, it can inspire others to do the same. There are many different things that you can do to keep the legacy of your loved one alive. For example, friends participate in an annual Alzheimer's walk to honor their grandmother who suffered from this disease. Others have set up foundations and organizations to help others who have been bullied or suffer from depression.

I woke up very sad on the first birthday after Bill died. As I cried in the shower, I had the inspiration to declare it as Billy Joe Sebastian Day. I posted on Facebook and asked others to remember Bill and honor his legacy by doing something he loved doing. It was a day to share his legacy as a taco lover, a good listener, someone who paid for someone else's meal or left an exorbitant tip for the wait staff. These are all actions that exemplify Bill's legacy. This day has grown and spread even to people who never knew him personally. A very sad day has transformed into a joyful one as I look forward to hearing back from those who remember the best qualities of a great man who blessed others.

## RECONNECT THROUGH MUSIC

Sometimes you simply hear the introduction to a song and you are ready to sing all the lyrics. Beyond that, you are transported to another time and place with someone you love. That's the power of music. Make a list of the favorite songs you shared with your loved one. What memories do these songs elicit? Create a playlist of these songs and share with those closest to your loved one along with an explanation of why these songs make you remember him/her now.

## DISCOVER CREATIVE EXPRESSIONS

Gather the family together and see if you can remember the funniest joke, a great story, a favorite saying, a quirky expression, etc. Start a shared journal you pass around to family members and/or friends where each person can add their favorite one. When feeling sad, channel the pain to creative expressions as a way to create a legacy to remember the loved one who has died.

Here's a partial list of creative options:

- Scrapbook
- Poem
- Song
- Journal
- Blog
- Video
- Mind map
- Doodles
- Give-away of treasured possessions
- Slideshow
- Photo book

## TAKE A MEMORIAL TRIP

Bill loved road trips. We often joked that he had 'itchy feet.' He enjoyed the planning stages of where he wanted to go and who we would visit almost as much as taking the actual trip. One of his life goals was to take all the grandkids to California to see the places where he grew up and where we got married, and to let them experience the beauty of the mountains and the beach. The summer after his death, I took the family to California to fulfill this dream. What an honor to revisit the places that shaped him and that he had talked about his whole life! Here are the steps that we took to plan and take the Billy Joe Sebastian Memorial Road Trip:

- Make a list of significant places to visit
- Share the list with the family and let them add and expand
- Write down any stories or anecdotes connected with specific places
- Put a physical map on a bulletin board and put stick pins where you want to go
- List and contact friends who would want to honor his/her life
- Plan a trip around these places and journal as you go there
- Make a slideshow using the pictures that you take of these places
- Make a video of feelings and comments when visiting significant places

## PRAYER

Thank You, Lord, that I can choose to honor the legacy of _____. I am grateful for his/her life and the lessons he/she taught me. Give me ears to listen to what You will say to me in this difficult place. You promise to give peace to your people and I receive it now (Psalm 85:8).

Give me creative ways to rekindle memories that identify the essence of _____'s legacy so many can also benefit from his/her life and experiences. Thank You for adjusting my priorities so that I can remember what he/she taught me through words and example. We know that his/her life message can bless future generations (Proverbs 4:13 TLB).

Teach me to honor and respect everyone in my life while they are still living (I Peter 2:17 NKJV). Grant wisdom on ways to continue to honor them after they are no longer physically with us. Give me grace to hold on tight to the confession of my hope without any signs of wavering. I long to keep a firm grip on the promises that are in Your Word. Give me understanding to encourage and help others out so that our lives become a worship song as we love one another (Hebrews 10:23-25 NASB).

In Jesus' name. Amen.

## HOPE EXPRESSIONS

*Be devoted to one another in love.*
*Honor one another above yourselves.*
*Romans 12:10*

# Discovering What (Not) to Say

*Singing light songs to the heavyhearted is like pouring salt in their wounds. Proverbs 25:20 MSG*

This chapter deals with well-meaning people who have no idea how to help those who are going through mourning after a death. They mean well and really want to help the one who is in pain, yet so many times they can say things that hang in the air and even create a rift. If you relate to the contents of this chapter, share it with those closest to you in order to guide them in the best ways to help you.

A few months after my husband died, I ran into a friend from church at the grocery store.

"Are you over the hump yet?" she asked.

I know she had good intentions, yet her words left me shaking my head. I completely ignored her question and turned my attention to her nametag that indicated that she was now working at the store.

"How long have you been working here?" I replied.

"Well, didn't you lose your husband recently?" she continued.

"So are you working here in the flower department?" I asked her, because that is another one of my least favorite expressions.

"Yes, I am. Are you okay?" she kept on.

"I'm doing great. Good luck with your new job. See you soon," I replied as I rushed to get as far away from her as possible.

For many of us, these are uncharted waters because people don't feel comfortable talking about death. We live in a society that struggles with what to say in the face of tragedy—particularly the death of a loved one. Because we're uncomfortable with the whole subject, we feel that we must be strong and stoic. This leads to a process of stuffing our emotions and choking back tears. As a result, we fumble for the right words to comfort someone who is going through a hard time. Sometimes it's so far out of our comfort zone that we avoid the person altogether. It's an awkward topic where we don't know what to say or, worse yet, say nothing at all.

Some people will want to make sure that you know that you should not be sad because your loved one is in a better place. This super spirituality is like having a glass of cold water splashed in your face when you are hurting. Every single one of the statements are true, yet come across as if the person who comes to comfort is trying to make themselves feel better rather than focusing on your suffering. These types of statements that seek to get others to see things from the positive side do not give real hope. Real hope comes from the Lord as you adjust to life without your loved one by your side.

## PROVIDE COMFORT

Many questions go unanswered when terrible things happen to wonderful people. It can feel like there is no justice and that can leave us stranded in our faith. Faith doesn't come in a neat, logical formula. Many feel that their job in comforting a person who is going through difficult times is to make them feel better. The word 'comfort' in Greek means to 'come alongside.' When Jesus tells

His disciples that He will be going away, He tells them that He will send them the Holy Spirit who is 'the comforter.' The best way to provide comfort is to be with the person who is going through the valley of despair and allow the Holy Spirit to comfort them from the inside out.

Those who have walked a similar path can provide true comfort and encouragement as they listen first and share with great empathy at appropriate times. It's important to come with the purpose to be a blessing rather than having all the answers and providing a quick fix. Keep in mind that each person works through their pain and loss in different ways and at a unique pace.

## AVOID THE FOLLOWING CLICHÉS

Below is a list of phrases to avoid when speaking to someone who recently experienced the death of their loved one.

"I know how you feel."

You don't know how I feel. I'm not even sure how I feel. Even if your loss was similar, you don't know what I'm going through. Each person's mourning experience is unique, so don't presume to know what they are feeling.

"Are you over it yet?"

Most people who say this mean well and want you to adjust to what they consider 'normal' life. Reality is that the mourning process is messy and you can't make a list and check off your progress. I will never get over Bill's death nor do I want to. I shared many years with this man, and he will always be a part of who I am. At the right time, I will know that I have walked through the valley of the shadow of death and have come out on the other end.

"He's in a better place."

This is a logical and common expression that also has good intentions. The reality is that, as I grieve, I don't want to hear it. I want my loved one here with me.

"God must have loved them more or needed a _____ (fill in the blank with their skill)."

This particular statement leaves us empty because what does that mean about those of us left behind? For the person reeling from personal loss, these words are empty and could be offensive.

"I'm sure you're glad he/she isn't suffering anymore."

I may not have come to terms with the fact of why he suffered in the first place. My head knows this to be true, but right now I want him here with me. Also, this can make me feel guilty. It is best to let the person who is mourning express this.

"At least you had him/her for so many years."

This statement is an attempt to put a positive spin on a sad situation. It is one thing to agree with someone who says it and quite another to be the one attempting to make someone feel better. How many years is long enough to have a person you love so much? This statement seems to want to talk the person out of being sad for no longer having their loved one in their life.

"God never gives us more than we can handle."

These words are not found anywhere in the Bible. The scripture used as the reference point for this platitude (1 Corinthians 10:13) is talking about temptation and not grief. When you tell a person this, it leaves them feeling either that they are weak or that God is mean and overbearing.

"You now have an angel watching over you."

I have wonderful memories of my husband, yet he is not my personal angel. He is in the presence of the Lord and one day I will see him again when I join him in that wonderful place. The Holy Spirit is my comforter and will give me the consolation I need to adjust to this life change.

"It must be a relief to no longer have to care for him."

As a long-term caregiver, I was often weary, but it was a privilege to care for my husband. I would have gladly continued in the process and considered it a blessing. I didn't know what to say to the person who said this to me. I wanted to hit them. Instead, I mumbled something and got as far away from them as quickly as I could. Thinking back on my reaction, I realize that they probably didn't mean it to come out the way that it did.

"What are you going to do now?"

I have no idea what I'm going to do. I have to learn how to navigate my life without this loved one. Don't put me on the spot by asking this question. I know I'm not going to make any hasty decisions except for the one to stop talking to you if you keep pushing.

## WHAT TO SAY

Perhaps while looking over the list of ten things not to say, you realized that those were the things that you always say to someone who is grieving the death of a loved one. So what should you say?

"I am sad too."

Once I got home, I began to call those closest to me to tell them about Bill. The most comforting response was when they cried with me as it instructs in Romans 12:15b (ISV): "Cry with those who are crying." They rode the waves of sorrow with me.

"I remember when . . ."

We crave hearing stories and the way that our loved one made a difference in the lives of others. Facebook was a blessing because many of Bill's friends wrote about the crazy things they had done in their youth. It brought tears and a smile every time.

Say nothing and listen.

One of the best things to do is to ask, "Is there anything I can do?" Then listen with compassion and caring. This is not the time to give practical advice. Resist the temptation to tell your story. Give them a listening ear and a tender heart. Offer them a shoulder to cry on and a hug when they most need it.

Reach out to them in the coming weeks.

A lot of people will call and visit right after a funeral. A few weeks or months later, few will take the time to do that. We realize that life goes on for everyone else, but it means the world when someone reaches out and touches us with kindness in the months afterwards. Send a card. Leave a message. Let us know that you are praying for us on a consistent basis. Best of all, spend time with us.

# Hope Tools

The most important part of coming alongside someone who is hurting is to take action. We show we care when we consistently reach out to the person who has experienced a loss. Here are some ways to do this.

## MAKE CALLS

Be prepared that the person who is grieving may not answer their phone in the first few days after a loss. Leave a warm, heartfelt message of support and love with the added gift of telling them you will call back in a week or so. If you don't know the person well, follow up the call with a card. If you are close, be sure to keep your promise to call back at a better time. Also, when they answer, always ask them if this is a good time to talk. Keep your call brief.

## Send Cards

Write a personal note when sending a card. One of the best parts about notes is that they provide a long-term source of comfort because they can be reread repeatedly. Share your feelings candidly, yet focus mainly on the person who has suffered, who survived the loss. Here are a few ideas to get you started:

"I cannot even imagine what you are going through right now..."

"This must be difficult for you..."

"My heart broke when I heard about..."

"I was devastated when I heard the news..."

Express how you feel. Let them know you are there for them. Make it about them. Write and send these cards consistently. With all the electronic communication at our fingertips, it's also a great idea to utilize emails, texting, and/or messaging to reach out to those who are grieving. Be sensitive not to overwhelm him/her and at the same time provide consistent support.

There is a flurry of attention and care immediately after a death. This dies down quickly as everyone returns to their normal lives. This can actually be the very best time to send a card with a personal note. Include a story or interesting quote that you remember about the one who died. This extra effort is guaranteed to bring a tear, a smile, or even a chuckle.

## ASK QUESTIONS – THEN LISTEN

After my father-in-law died, I spent hours listening to my mother-in-law reminisce about their life together. I never fully understood the value of a good listening ear until my own husband died. It is a huge comfort to remember our wonderful times together. I enjoy asking my children about their favorite memories of their dad.

Listening is a rare gift that can make a huge difference in processing grief. It requires being present in the moment and the sharing of your time and life. Be on the lookout for opportunities to practice your listening skills with those who are mourning. Here are some conversation starters:

- Do you remember when_____?
- What do you miss most?
- What's the funniest joke_____ ever told or prank _____ played on someone else?
- What was his/her favorite saying?
- What do you remember about the last trip you took together?

Let them talk (or not). Remember that silence is golden as they struggle to put words around their feelings. Listen quietly, thoughtfully, and without interrupting. Resist the temptation to tell your own stories and give them the time to process their emotions. Align your body language with your desire to listen. You do this by maintaining natural eye contact, keeping an open posture, and leaning forward to show that you are engaged. If your mind tends to wander, ask for permission to doodle and/or take notes. When the conversation ends, hand them your notes to reflect on later. They can even put it in their memory book.

A good listener shows empathy by making feeling statements. Empathetic responses draw out the feelings of others. Be wary of saying that you understand their pain or what they have gone through. A better way to express your shared sorrow is to say something like, "That must be very hard for you. I can only imagine how painful that must be now."

Keep in mind that your goal as a listener is to give the gift of your time. Nothing makes a person feel more valued and nurtured than being 'heard.' This is not the time to offer advice or judge their progress in the grief journey. Listening is a treasure that costs you nothing except awareness and focus on the needs of someone else. Listening during this time of grieving is priceless.

## PRAYER

Lord, give me wisdom to pick the right words to say when comforting someone who is starting a grief journey. Give me a heart of compassion and deep empathy so I can come alongside as others go through the hard times. I know that You have been teaching me how this feels so I can be there for others just as You have been there for me (2 Corinthians 1:3-5 MSG).

Lord, thank You for all those who have prayed for me and listened to me during this time of sorrow. I am grateful for the understanding You give me in my own journey to be able to speak life into the painful situations that others face (Proverbs 18:21). I know there will be much fruit from the loving words that I can speak into the lives of others. Thank You for providing opportunities to listen to those who are hurting.

I ask You, Lord, to give me the words to say to others who are mourning. Give me Your loving words that flow from a heart that hurts with those who are hurting. If

I'm in doubt, guide me to say nothing rather than offend. Lord, set a watch before my mouth and guard me from my own discomfort (Matthew 12:36-37). I pray that I can show Your love in tangible ways that reassure the one who is suffering that You are a good God. I know that You will meet them in the very place of their suffering and provide exactly what they need.

In Jesus' name. Amen.

## HOPE EXPRESSIONS

*Be happy with those who are happy, and weep with those who weep.*
*Romans 12:15 NLT*

# Letting Go

I can't believe that it was such a hard decision to make. I feared mentioning it to anyone because even as I tried to articulate the words, they sounded foolish.

I carried the phone bill in my purse for a month, meaning to make the call to cancel my husband's phone. I missed hearing his voice, and so, on days when I was overwhelmed with missing him, I dialed his number and waited to hear the recording. The intonation as he said his name . . . Bill Sebastian . . . always made me smile.

As I placed the call, I felt the tears starting to pool behind my eyes. I almost hung up as I had so many times before.

"Hello, my name is Rachel. How can I help you?"

"I need to cancel my husband's phone because he. . . he moved four months ago," I stuttered.

"Does he want to keep his number?" she asked.

"Oh no, I wasn't clear. He moved to Heaven and no longer needs his phone," I replied, choking back tears.

"Oh, I am so sorry for your loss, ma'am," she answered kindly.

It took a few moments for me to regain my composure in order to continue to tell her what I needed to do.

"Ma'am, I wanted to let you know that we could just suspend that phone and you could reactivate it at any time," she assured me. "Here's what we can do. It will take me a few minutes to access your account and verify the status. Let's wait until the very end of our call and you can let me know then if you want to suspend the account or cancel it," she offered.

As I waited on hold, I walked over to the window and glanced out at the stark outline of our large oak tree. I remembered the small sapling we inherited when we bought this house.

*Where did the time go?* I thought to myself. My mind flashed to a kaleidoscope of memories of the challenges and good times we had shared. Through it all, the tree had continued to grow. Each fall it shed its leaves and grew stronger against the wind. *Much like our family.*

"So sorry this is taking so long," came the voice on

the other end of the line.

Wiping a tear, I cleared my throat and said, "Oh, that's okay."

I stared out the window again and saw a few lonely leaves fall to the ground. They were the ones which seemed to have hung on after the others had floated to the ground. My tears began to fall as well.

*I just miss him so much! How can I go on?* I thought to myself.

And then I saw it . . . one little leaf at the very top of the tree. The cold wind was blowing and yet it continued to hang on. It seemed to wave at me as if to get my attention.

"It's lonely up here. I'm cold and shaky," the leaf seemed to say.

I'd been hanging on . . . calling that number just to hear the familiar voice. I cried every time I heard it.

I felt the Lord speak to my heart, *Trust Me and let go. You don't need technology to help you remember. You recognize My voice, and I used Bill as a vessel to teach you My loving voice.*

I gazed out the window and at that precise second the last little leaf that had been hanging on so tenaciously to the branch floated down to the ground. I know that plants can't talk, but it seemed like it was saying, "This is fun. Look at me travel. If I let go, you can too!"

"Ma'am, I am so sorry to make you wait. Have you decided what you want to do with the phone?" she asked.

"I want you to cancel that phone," I told her.

I felt a great sense of peace as I finished out the final details of the call. Like the little leaf, I was letting go. In a way, I have been letting go a little bit at a time and picking up the pieces of my new life. There is a sadness when letting go until you realize that the memories grow sweeter as you cherish them.

When a loved one dies, the grief can seem overwhelming. Initially, the pain is eased by the busyness of attending to details and having others around. The scenario changes when everyone leaves and you are left alone. You begin your year of firsts. Every time that you approach a birthday or special holiday, there can be additional pain around the fact that your loved one is not there. Each person has their own unique grief journey and the timing that goes with it varies. At some point, however, you will feel like it is time to let go of the past.

Letting go does not mean that you forget about your loved one. Deep sorrow does not keep their memory alive. The beautiful, wonderful memories will always remain. You can begin a new volume of your life knowing that the past you had with your loved one marked you forever. That dear one helped make you who you are. The memories you shared will never be erased and can be cherished. You never let go of the person, but you do have to let go of the life you shared with them.

# Hope Tools

## GO THROUGH THE STUFF

The day before my husband's memorial service, my daughters helped me clear out the medical supplies and various apparatuses that filled our home. We packed up all of Bill's beloved Hawaiian shirts and put the rest of his clothing into boxes to take to the local charity. This was a huge help. I was able to put a check mark next to at least one item on my long to-do list. It also was part of the process of accepting the finality that he no longer needed them. On top of that, it gave my kids a chance to begin to process their grief as well. Each one had a very different approach to how they wanted to help. I released them to do whatever they felt they wanted to do. Just the fact that they were there meant the world to me.

In my own situation, it was fine for my children to come in to pack up their dad's belongings, clean the bathrooms, and run errands. For some it can be healthy to begin to sort through stuff quickly. For others who are not ready yet, it may be too difficult to move forward in this area immediately. The main thing is to keep making progress rather than let grief paralyze you. No matter when you start, going through the belongings of the one who died is a necessary part of the mourning process. With it comes the realization that your life has changed.

Take a layering approach if you feel overwhelmed. Tackle one closet at a time. You do not have to get this done in a day. It would not be wise to do so. Get your calendar and set timed goals as to what you will do and when. Get an accountability partner to help you. Set the one-year anniversary as your benchmark to finish going through the physical things.

Find a special place to put the items you want to keep. Bill was an avid collector of Western memorabilia.

He collected it gradually for over thirty years and took great joy in displaying it. It was difficult for him to part with any piece of his collection. I had been feeling panicky at the thought of going through all of his treasures, but then a dear friend told me she plans to start a Cowboy Television Station. She has agreed to let me set up the Billy Joe Sebastian Memorial Cowboy Museum. I will be able to display his best items, and others who love cowboys can also enjoy them. This plan brings me joy because it honors his love for his childhood memorabilia and continues his legacy.

## Look Forward to a Bright Future

The death of your loved one changed your life forever. If you have worked through the Hope Tools in this book, you have been empowered to work through the pain and sadness. You have acknowledged your grief, embraced your pain, and maintained hope in the process.

In Psalm 23:4, we have a familiar verse that tells us, "Even though I walk through the valley of the shadow of death I will fear no evil." I've quoted that verse many times, yet had never focused on the fact that we walk through the valley. We don't get stuck there or run the other way. The great news about this verse is that it shows that we can get through the valley of grief and pain, especially if we hold on to the hope that we are not moving into this valley forever.

At first you feel that your life is over. Death rips your heart out, yet God is always near. Perhaps you have already started experiencing a new level of peace Jesus promised when He said, "Peace I leave with you; my peace I give you. I do not give to you as the world gives. Do not let your hearts be troubled and do not be afraid" (John 14:27). While it is true that one part of your life ends when a loved one dies, you are still alive. This can be a difficult transition as you redefine your role and develop the confidence you need to move forward.

Once you have faced your grief and feel ready to move forward, it's important to step back and take stock of all that God has done for you. Brainstorm the next steps of where you are headed. While it is good to plan, it's important to be obedient in little things and let the Lord fight your battles. God fights for you—rest at peace in Him as He takes care of all enemies. Stand or move forward doing what God has called you to do, and He will fight your battles. Be obedient in little things to be positioned for larger breakthroughs.

## REDEFINE YOUR ROLE

I look back over the last three years and can see how far I have come. I recall the sinking feeling I felt the first time that I had to acknowledge that I was a widow. I called the Social Security office to let them know that Bill had died.

"Are you Bill Sebastian's widow?" the voice on the phone asked me.

"Yes, I am," I replied.

I could barely finish the call and sobbed when I hung up the phone. I did not choose this change in my life. After Bill died, I had a hard time adjusting to the fact that I was no longer a full-time caregiver. It was even harder to realize that I was no longer a wife. Instead, I was a widow. I had a choice. As I entered into the valley of the shadow of death, I could choose to camp out there or I could continue to take steps toward my new future. The Holy Spirit was very close and I felt great comfort. It is a wonderful thing to fully embrace the pain and deal with the anguish of moving forward without your life's partner. I could take on the identity of a grieving widow or I could begin to redefine my role and purpose in life.

Grace abounded as I released my grief and discovered the strength to find joy again. At first, I loved to tell about my journey as a widow and the miracles I had seen along the way. Gradually, however, I began to see the need to redefine my statements. I decided to work on my unique Hope Identity Statement that I could use when meeting someone.

Here's a list of questions that I put in my journal that helped me to define my future:

- Who are you?

- What brings you great joy and purpose?

- What captures your attention and brings a great sense of satisfaction?

- What are you uniquely qualified to do?

- What have you always wanted to do?

- What would you need to do in order to become qualified to do what you most want to do?

- So what? Why does this make a difference? What motivates you to do what you do?

I modeled it after the 30-second elevator speech that we use when networking.

Hope Identity Template:

My name is _____. I am a _____. I passionately pursue (love to) _____ so that _____.

Here's my example using that template:

My name is Karen Sebastian. I am an author and speaker. I passionately pursue opportunities to share the light of hope in dark places so that others can benefit from the rich insights gained in my grief journey after the death of my husband.

## DEVELOP CONFIDENCE

Did you answer that first question with what you do for a living or one of your roles? Dig deep to discover your identity and what you believe about yourself. Strike the words 'just' from your description. Practice your Hope Identity Statement in front of the mirror. Pretend that you are meeting someone for the first time. Smile and make eye contact as you make this your answer every time that you get the question, "What do you do?"

Most of us live by default because we stay on a certain path and do the things that make us the most comfortable. As you step out of your comfort zone, you will need to move boldly and with confidence. This confidence comes from discovering your purpose and taking steps every day toward that future. They do not have to be huge steps, yet they should be consistent. Expect to feel slightly uncomfortable as you take each one. Each step moves you toward a change in your thinking and should be celebrated.

Embracing grief allows you to reconsider your priorities. You get to see firsthand how fleeting life can be. None of us has a guaranteed ride, and we need to make every moment count in making a difference. It's a wonderful time for a change. It's a great opportunity to do what you've always longed to do but found yourself unable to dedicate the time and effort toward. As the fog lifts, you can begin to see endless possibilities. There is new territory for you to conquer. There's no limit to what you can do in the days ahead. Go for your dreams!

As you move forward to fulfilling your dream, plan a getaway where you can spend quality time working on your Hope Identity Statement and developing a vision for the future. This is a wonderful time to explore places you've always wanted to go. Begin to plan an overnight or weekend trip alone. This break from your routine will help you push that 'reset' button.

As you start the process of going for your dream, treat it as if you were preparing to run a marathon. You would start with small exercises and runs. You would commit to daily progress with diligence and consistency. You would begin slowly, yet keep the ultimate goal of running the marathon in the forefront of your mind. You would build your stamina gradually as you pace yourself. On the day of the marathon, you would be ready to succeed.

If it seems far too daunting to take a trip alone, seek to go on a spiritual retreat. There are many available through churches and other organizations. The most important thing is for you to put your focus on writing your Hope Identity Statement. What are the broken pieces of your most recent grief experience? What insights have you learned in this process? What can you do to make a difference in the lives of others? List some steps that will take you in the right direction and start taking them.

There is no waste in God's economy. You have been through a hard season that seemed like it would never end. You made it through the valley of the shadow of death. As you emerge, you are stronger, wiser, and have a better perspective of your own opportunities for the future.

## PRAYER

I am so grateful for Your grace and mercy during this time of sorrow. This has been a hard journey, yet one where You have walked with me every step of the way. I know You will give me the strength to overcome my current challenges as You teach me the next steps to take to move forward. Teach me to recognize Your voice (John 10:27 MSG). Even though I can't hear Your audible voice, You guide me through the impressions and thoughts You give. Lord, thank You for allowing me the privilege to hear Your sweet voice during times of decision. Grant me wisdom to continue recognizing Your voice and letting go in order to allow Your comfort to flow into my life.

I am grateful for all the blessings You've given me throughout my life and for Your loving kindness that is new every morning. You have truly been a refuge during this grief journey and have been my strength (Psalm 59:16-17). I trust You to continue to provide abundantly.

Help me to remember that while _____ died, I did not. Grant me the grace to pick up the pieces of my broken heart and continue to live as I come out of the dark shadows of grief into the rest of my life (Psalm 23:4).

## HOPE EXPRESSIONS

*Praise be to the God and Father of our Lord Jesus Christ, the Father of compassion and the God of all comfort, who comforts us in all our troubles, so that we can comfort those in any trouble with the comfort we ourselves receive from God.*
*2 Corinthians 1:3-4*

*Surely the righteous will never be shaken; they will be remembered forever. They will have no fear of bad news; their hearts are steadfast, trusting in the Lord. Their hearts are secure, they will have no fear; in the end they will look in triumph on their foes.*
*Psalm 112:6-8*

# *Afterword*

I think it best to let Bill finish this book which was inspired by his life and faith despite the challenges and even death. This was one of the last verses that my husband, Bill, shared on his Facebook page. It testifies of his faith and confidence that God is the true source of all hope no matter what happens.

*From such terrible dangers of death he saved us, and will save us; and we have placed our hope in him that he will save us again, as you help us by means of your prayers for us. So it will be that the many prayers for us will be answered, and God will bless us; and many will raise their voices to him in thanksgiving for us.*
*2 Corinthians 1:10 - 11 GNT*

God will protect us. He will save us!! Love it!!

# Karen Sebastian

### Author | International Speaker | Hope Catalyst
*Shining the light of hope into dark places*

Karen Sebastian believes God brings the light of hope into the darkest hours of our lives. Driven by her personal journey from despair to hope, Karen candidly shares her heart and the adventures of discovering the beauty of 'hope rays' on dark cloudy days. She has experienced first-hand that life may not be easy when you face challenges you never 'signed up for.' It's in these dark places that the light of hope can illuminate the possibilities and bring you into unexpected venues of promise. Her powerful books offer refreshing Biblical perspectives, allowing you to receive and impart God's gift of hope.

Rather than dealing with issues of rebellion, *The Power of Hope for Prodigals* helps you see your prodigal from God's perspective, enabling you to speak life and experience the transforming power of hope.

*The Power of Hope in Mourning* teaches you to 'ride' the waves of grief so that the very pain that threatens to destroy you pushes you into the presence of God where hope and healing await.

*Karen Sebastian explains from experience the enormity of the possible when hope seems dim. . .* **– Jack W. Hayford**, Pastor/Author/Hymn writer

Karen Sebastian is a dynamic and gifted speaker who shares from the rich experiences of her life. She has faced many challenges that could cause despair—serious health issues, infertility, a prodigal daughter, caring for her disabled spouse, and recently becoming a widow. She shares from her heart how God gave her transforming hope to not just survive these difficult situations, but to overcome and enjoy an abundant life even before the circumstances changed.

Karen will inspire you, teach you, make you laugh and cry as she brings the light of hope found in God's Word, coupled with practical ways to release this transforming power of God in your life. You will love her transparent vulnerability and feel empowered to face life's challenges with courage and hope.

Karen is fluent in Spanish, having grown up as a missionary in Latin America. She is an ordained minister who served as co-pastor of several churches alongside her husband. She also has been a corporate trainer for over 25 years where she has shared the message of hope in many venues including training seminars and webinars for Fortune 500 companies. Karen founded HOPEpreneurs, a consulting firm that helps women succeed in the marketplace through hope-filled strategic planning.

**Contact Information:**
Karen is available for seminars, conferences, retreats, and banquets. She travels from Dallas, TX. For more information email karen@karensebastian.com

 /hopeispowerful  karensebastian  ./karensebastian1

46698654R00089

Made in the USA
Charleston, SC
18 September 2015